Also by Michael Adams

Sex in the Snow
Canadian Social Values at the End of the Millennium

Better Happy than Rich?
Canadians, Money and the Meaning of Life

Fire and Ice
The United States, Canada, and the Myth of Converging Values

American Backlash

THE UNTOLD STORY OF SOCIAL CHANGE IN
THE UNITED STATES

MICHAEL ADAMS

WITH AMY LANGSTAFF AND DAVID JAMIESON

VIKING
CANADA

VIKING CANADA

Published by the Penguin Group

Penguin Group (Canada), 90 Eglinton Avenue East, Suite 700, Toronto, Ontario,
Canada M4P 2Y3 (a division of Pearson Penguin Canada Inc.)

Penguin Group (USA) Inc., 375 Hudson Street, New York, New York 10014, U.S.A.
Penguin Books Ltd, 80 Strand, London WC2R 0RL, England
Penguin Ireland, 25 St Stephen's Green, Dublin 2, Ireland (a division of Penguin Books Ltd)
Penguin Group (Australia), 250 Camberwell Road, Camberwell, Victoria 3124, Australia
(a division of Pearson Australia Group Pty Ltd)
Penguin Books India Pvt Ltd, 11 Community Centre, Panchsheel Park, New Delhi – 110 017,
India
Penguin Group (NZ), cnr Airborne and Rosedale Roads, Albany, Auckland 1310, New Zealand
(a division of Pearson New Zealand Ltd)
Penguin Books (South Africa) (Pty) Ltd, 24 Sturdee Avenue, Rosebank, Johannesburg 2196,
South Africa

Penguin Books Ltd, Registered Offices: 80 Strand, London WC2R 0RL, England

First published 2005

1 2 3 4 5 6 7 8 9 10   (FR)

Copyright © Michael Adams, 2005

Author representation: Westwood Creative Artists
94 Harbord Street, Toronto, Ontario M5S 1G6

Manufactured in Canada.

LIBRARY AND ARCHIVES CANADA CATALOGUING IN PUBLICATION

Adams, Michael, 1946 Sept. 29–
American backlash : the untold story of social change in the U.S. / Michael Adams.

ISBN 0-670-06370-3

1. Social change—United States. 2. United States—Social conditions—1980–
3. United States—Relations—Foreign countries. I. Title.

HN59.2.A32 2005   973.931   C2005-903128-X

Visit the Penguin Group (Canada) website at **www.penguin.ca**

For my colleagues at Environics, past, present, and future

Contents

Preface

I WAS BORN in a small Ontario town in 1946, the product of a mixed marriage between a Roman Catholic mother and Protestant father, both of whom are still alive and still in love. In the mid 1950s we moved to the big city, Toronto, for the economic opportunity it afforded.

After I more or less mastered the four Rs, including the catechism of my religion, I developed a love for school. This love came about mainly because of the history and languages I learned there, especially the English language. In university I became a young Progressive Conservative, Canada's unique political oxymoron, in defiance of a family tradition that had boasted a Liberal member of Parliament.

I studied political science and sociology when my smartest friends read economics and the law. I wanted to know what people thought and why they behaved the way they did. In retrospect, I was a curious contrarian, always in my heart admiring that little boy in the fairy tale who was the first to see that the emperor had no clothes.

Fortunately, in addition to being contrary in my youth, I was also entrepreneurial. In graduate school in 1970 I co-founded the polling and market research company, Environics, that has given me my livelihood and served as a lifelong vehicle of my post-graduate education. This path has led me to my current self-appointed status as author-in-residence after a publisher friend urged me to write a book in the mid 1990s about my life's work, the study of social values.

This book, my fourth, focuses on social change in the United States of America.

Not so long ago the United States was the most admired nation on the planet, the first nation among equals, leading humankind into the future. Now it is the world's only superpower, first in economic and military might but no longer, international polls attest, first in the hearts of the world. America has always been exceptional. In the middle of the twentieth century that exceptionalism seemed a beacon to many nations; today it seems to many, including half of America's own engaged citizens, to be leading America in a problematic direction. This book is about that trajectory. It documents a surprising and radical change in the mental posture of the American people since the 1970s, one that has taken a fascinating tack since that terrible day known as 9/11.

My goal in this book is to describe American values, not to judge them. Of course, you the reader are the final judge of my take on the world's most exciting country in a daunting, often dangerous world.

July 1, 2005

Introduction

In 2004 a small crisis occurred in Spurger, Texas (population: 1,000). A controversy arose around the school district's annual TWIRP day, a homecoming tradition that school officials said had been going on for years, maybe even generations. TWIRP stands for The Woman Is Requested to Pay. On TWIRP day girls would ask boys on dates, open doors for them, treat them to a milkshake or a burger, and generally woo them as the boys themselves would usually woo the girls (or might have in the 1950s). In the spirit of the day, boys and girls would sometimes playfully don the clothing of the opposite sex: football players dressed as cheerleaders and the like.

But no more. In November 2004 concerned parents complained that the event encouraged homosexuality by inviting young people to transgress gender norms. As one mother said, "It's like experimenting with drugs. You just keep playing with it and it becomes customary."

School officials in Spurger expressed surprise that such a seemingly benign tradition should cause upset, but were conciliatory. Rather than have the few parents who complained seek excused absences for their children on "moral grounds," Spurger schools ditched TWIRP day altogether. The model of the Salem witch trials is repeated often enough: a latent cultural anxiety is harnessed by a few zealous individuals who are able to bring about considerable change, fuelled not so much by reason or political clout as by communal fear and uncertainty. But while Spurger officials were willing to give up TWIRP day, it didn't seem fair to get rid of a festive occasion students had enjoyed without offering some alternative. The replacement? Camo Day, on which boys and girls alike dress up in military garb: camouflage, combat boots, face paint, perhaps a plastic grenade or two. While cross-dressing presented a challenge to the sensibilities of some Spurger residents, there were no reports of conscientious objectors being kept home on Camo Day.

To some Americans, the Spurger story probably seems sadly emblematic of the trajectory of American society. For progressive Americans, who have stood amazed at the political realignment that has seen conservative Republicans gain so much ground in the legislative arena (where they have duly voiced their rage about everything from Janet Jackson's right nipple to purportedly gay SpongeBob SquarePants), a dress-up day turning from a social role–playing game to a military-themed event must look depressingly exemplary. In a column in the *Detroit Free Press,* Mitch Albom, author of the pop spirituality bestsellers *Tuesdays with Morrie* and *The Five People You Meet in Heaven,* argued that Spurger's gay panic was overblown, but that there might be something more serious to worry about there. Albom reports the following conversation he had with a lawyer for one of the families who objected to TWIRP day:

> "Isn't camouflage gear associated with killing things—at the very least, animals, at the very worst, human beings?" I asked Sasser, the attorney. "What do you think about a 4-year-old dressing in camouflage?"
>
> "We have no problem with that," he said.
>
> *That's* something to worry about.

Even setting aside Albom's objections, there are also those who, whatever their ideology, simply lament the vehemence of current debates on political and cultural matters. Responding to what he thought was over-the-top ideological criticism of his film *Million Dollar Baby,* Clint Eastwood remarked, "Maybe I'm getting to the age when I'm starting to be senile or nostalgic or both, but people are so angry now. You used to be able to disagree with people and still be friends. Now you hear these talk shows, and everyone who believes differently from you is a moron and an idiot—both on the right and the left." To Americans like Eastwood, the Spurger story must seem further evidence that things have gotten too acrimonious and too politicized. Why could the Spurgerites of the 1950s, surely not exactly a bunch of Texan Liberaces, enjoy TWIRP day while their grandchildren in 2004 see it as a moral affront?

Are these two reads on the TWIRP controversy accurate? Is American society indeed engaged in a culture war? And if so, is the conservative side winning and growing, as political developments would seem to suggest?

Let's deal first with the idea of the culture war, before we try to decide who's winning. In 1991 sociologist James Davison Hunter published a book entitled *Culture Wars: The Struggle to Define America*. The book argued that in America, two broad socio-political camps were emerging around such hot-button issues as guns, gays, abortion, prayer in schools— the now familiar litany. These two camps cut across some of the lines that had traditionally defined political affiliation, including religion and class. Increasingly, people's politics were defined not merely by their demographics (whether they were rich or poor, black or white, young or old), but by what Hunter called their world views. Essentially, Americans had entered the age of clashing values; the values consensus of mid-century could no longer be assumed. (Of that old consensus, Samuel Huntington, a prominent and conservative Harvard political scientist, remarked, "We were all liberals, and Franklin Roosevelt was God. I couldn't imagine that anyone thought differently.")

There is some debate over when the culture war was declared, but many trace its current incarnation to the Roe v. Wade decision in 1973 that aroused such an angry reaction from the anti-abortion camp. That anger, of course, has yet to abate: as George W. Bush nominates Supreme Court justices, religious Republicans are pushing hard for candidates who will undo the decision that has so incensed them for over three decades.

Just a year after Hunter's *Culture Wars* was published, Pat Buchanan gave a famous speech at the 1992 Republican convention. Buchanan, banished from the ticket but granted a prominent speaking role, spoke of a culture war that would shake the nation: "There is a religious war going on in this country," Buchanan boomed, "a cultural war as critical to the kind of nation we shall be as the Cold War itself, for this war is for the soul of America." George Bush Sr., the convention's kinder, gentler presidential nominee, was more moderate in his rhetoric. But he emerged from the 1992 convention as a candidate branded with two words that would help define the Republican Party throughout the culture war to come: family values.

Of course, family values didn't win the election for the Republicans that year. Bill Clinton was elected. He came, he saw, he triangulated (that is, he carved out a "third way" distinct from both Republican and Democratic ideology and party lines). He also, in his way, became one of the icons of the culture war. The Monica Lewinsky affair was a lightning rod for those alarmed by what they saw as America's moral decline: if even the president couldn't act with dignity in the highest office in the land, where was the nation headed? Polls showed that most Americans didn't much care about the president's *particular* indiscretion with "that woman." But if the media coverage it received was any indication, the affair seemed to have touched a tender nerve with the American people. Personal conduct, standards of propriety, and private and public morality became central topics of debate.

As the Clinton years ended, the slate of American books examining the so-called culture war grew long. Some of the titles speak to the binary terms of the dialogue: *One Nation, Two Cultures* (Gertrude Himmelfarb, 1999); *The Two Americas* (Stanley Greenberg, 2004); *Values Divide* (John White, 2002); *The Great Divide: Retro vs. Metro America* (John Sperling et al., 2004); *How to Win the Culture War* (Peter Kreeft, 2002). There have also been titles that questioned the by now dominant idea of a culture war: *One Nation, After All* (Alan Wolfe, 1999); *Culture War? The Myth of a Polarized America* (Morris P. Fiorina et al., 2005); *Is There a Culture War?* (Alan Wolfe and James Davison Hunter, forthcoming).

Social scientists, pollsters, politicos, journalists, and polemicists have all weighed in on the nature of the culture war, its fronts, and its likely outcomes. But for a war that's supposed to be about values, there's been relatively little empirical investigation of the values at stake. The same old polling numbers on abortion and gun control tend to be batted about endlessly.[1] The amazing growth of evangelicalism and megachurches is scrutinized, with some seeing a growing embrace of traditional values and others merely a population seeking support and social services anywhere they can be found. But perhaps the most discussed battle of all in the culture war is in the political arena, where Republicans and Democrats are supposed to be scarcely able to speak to one another, so shocked is each at the other's moral perfidy (Republicans are warmongering, xenophobic bigots, of course, while Democrats are America-hating narcissists whose self-indulgent quest for pleasure tramples everything decent people hold dear).

None of this information, however—polling, church membership, party affiliation—gets at the heart of Americans' values. These are all secondary indicators, behavioural or attitudinal data that flow from people's values but give us only partial information about the nature of those values.[2]

My firm has conducted social values studies in the United States every four years since 1992, around the time when discussions of a culture war as such hit the mainstream in America. In our four survey waves ('92, '96, '00, and '04) we have amassed 8,351 questionnaires completed by representative samples of Americans aged fifteen or older, each one with responses to over 600 questions on values.

Our surveys are not polls of people's opinions; rather, we seek to measure the deep values structures that underlie their opinions. While a poll might ask whether you favour same-sex marriage, our research measures the values that drive your position on same-sex marriage: your views on gender, family organization, religion, personal autonomy, and the role of the state.[3] Through computer number-crunching and human interpretation, we can combine all this data and gain insight into how people's values hang together to create a coherent world view, and how those world views relate to people's decisions in the world.

When we ask Americans directly about their values, not what church they attend or what candidate they support, what do we learn about the so-called culture war? For one thing, we find that whatever the culture war is, it is not a war between ordinary Republicans and average Democrats. When we look at the values of politically engaged Republicans and politically engaged Democrats, there are some differences between them, but there are also huge swaths of common ground.

On a personal level, Republicans and Democrats are quite similar in their efforts to exert control in their own lives. Both groups share a do-it-yourself approach to many areas of life, from proactive efforts to stay healthy to a desire to manage their own financial affairs with minimal assistance from professionals. Politically engaged Republicans and Democrats also share a strong work ethic, reporting more than the average American that they try hard to instill this value in their children. So we find that engaged citizens, regardless of their political persuasion, are more likely than average citizens to value making their own decisions and moving forward under their own steam.

When it comes to relating to others, we again find important similarities between engaged Republicans and engaged Democrats. Both groups are committed to some vision of community. While some differences emerge in what each group sees as the ideal community, there is consensus on three important pillars of public life: strong civic engagement, a deep belief in ethical behaviour as a foundation for relations with others, and an interest in taking time to connect emotionally with other people—whether family members, friends, neighbours, or even acquaintances.

On matters of social organization—the rules, both formal and informal, that should govern societies—Republicans and Democrats start to differ somewhat more. Both groups feel they have responsibilities toward the society in which they live, but they disagree on the nature of those responsibilities. Republicans on the whole stress patriotism and duty, while Democrats stress fairness and equality. These similarities and differences will be discussed in greater detail in Chapter 2.

Despite these differences in approach, the values of politically engaged Democrats and Republicans indicate agreement on a number of fundamental issues. Moreover, where differences arise, they certainly don't appear drastic enough to constitute anything resembling a "war."

So if Republicans and Democrats are having such a love-in, why does the political climate seem so acrimonious? Where did the idea of the culture war come from? Part of the culture war is, of course, a matter of representation. Conflict sells, and flipping on the TV to watch a couple of informed, thoughtful, conciliatory people developing pragmatic solutions to policy problems on which they differ … well, it might sound like heaven to a few cerebral souls, but it's unlikely to drive ratings and advertising revenues through the roof. Rush "femi-Nazi" Limbaugh sells. Bill "Bush acts like a girl on the rag" Maher sells. Ann "invade their countries, kill their leaders, and convert them to Christianity" Coulter sells.

Daily Show host Jon Stewart made a famous appearance on CNN's *Crossfire* in which he literally begged the show's hosts, Tucker Carlson and Paul Begala, to change the show's format and tone and help uplift America's political dialogue. Implausible, to say the least, particularly for a show whose raison d'être is, well, crossfire. The scornful response Stewart received as he repeated over and over "Please stop. Please. You're hurting America. Stop, *please*" (I paraphrase) was testament to the problem he was speaking of. All Carlson could think to do was ask Stewart why he didn't use *his* show to uplift political dialogue. And so it goes.

But the culture war is not *all* sound and fury signifying nothing. There is indeed a values divide in America, with its strong religious and moralist elements on the one side and its famously hedonistic popular and consumer culture raising the bar of excess on the other. A values divide also emerges strongly in our data, but the armies of the culture war, we find, are not defined by their political affiliation.

While much of the culture-war rhetoric seems to suggest that, politically, there are two kinds of people in America, Republicans and Democrats, there are, in fact, three kinds of people: Republicans, Democrats, and those who don't vote. The third group is the largest. Since the late 1970s voter turnout in the United States has been a little more than half. In the 2004 election, turnout rose to 60 percent. But even at that, a little less than 30 percent of Americans voted for Kerry, a little more than 30 percent voted for Bush, and the plurality—nearly 40 percent— didn't show up. They stayed home, even in the face of an election that both sides called the most important in a generation.

When compared with the values of non-voters, the values of politically engaged Republicans and Democrats look virtually identical. It is between voters and non-voters that the real chasm lies. An example: earlier I mentioned that social organization is the area in which Republicans and

Democrats diverge most sharply. According to our data, Republicans place more emphasis on patriotism than Democrats do; that is, Republicans are well above average on the value we label *National Pride* while Democrats are just slightly above average. Meanwhile, Democrats feel strongly that they have an obligation to help those worse off than themselves, and that the rich should try to help the poor. On this value, which we label *Social Responsibility,* Democrats are well above average while Republicans are just slightly above average. But on *both* these trends, Americans who say they are unlikely to vote are far below average.

The values of the politically disengaged show a distinct lack of idealism; these Americans seem to reject both the Republican and the Democratic visions of the good life and the ideal community. They don't believe in the importance of a father-led home as Republicans do disproportionately, but neither do they embrace gender equality as Democrats do disproportionately. They don't embrace traditional, institutional religion as Republicans do, but neither do they report being attracted to more personalized forms of spiritual practice as Democrats are. They reject traditional values and social norms, but not because they embrace a dream of inclusion and tolerance—the politically disengaged disproportionately reject both the traditional and the progressive.

People who take the time to reflect on a vision for America, who talk about that vision with other people or listen to a discussion about it on television (even from a polemicist!), and who finally vote for their favourite candidate are people who could probably agree on a great deal. As it turns out, it's not so much the content of the vision that matters; it's caring to have a vision at all that really counts.

It isn't that the contest of conservative and progressive ideas and policies doesn't exist in America. Of course it does, and it's articulated around the clock through a thousand channels. The point is that that debate, the political debate, doesn't get at the most important values gap in American society—the gap between the engaged and the disengaged.

So what *do* America's politically disengaged care about? They can't reject everything. This brings us around to one of the two questions I posed earlier. The first question was whether there's a culture war. Our

"Don't ask, don't tell, don't give a crap—that's my contract with America."

values data show there is, but it isn't the one we might have expected. The second question was, If there is a culture war, who's winning—progressives or conservatives? The answer is neither. When we look at changes in Americans' values over time (from 1992, when we began our surveys, to the summer of 2004, just before President Bush was re-elected), it's not the values of the politically ascendant conservatives *or* the values of the politically challenged progressives that are growing most rapidly. The values that are showing the strongest growth in America—especially among youth—are the values of the politically disengaged.

What are these values? According to our data, the values showing the most pronounced growth in the United States from 1992 to 2004 fell into three categories: risk-taking and thrill-seeking, Darwinism and exclusion, and consumption and status-seeking.

On average, Americans report increasing attraction to the pursuit of strong jolts of sensation. These jolts might be derived from drugs or adrenaline-pumping activities like extreme sports, intense media experiences like ultra-realistic video games, or even the thrills (and spills) of gambling and financial risk-taking. The values of the average American also reveal a growing resignation to life in a world of dog-eat-dog competition: Americans increasingly register a Darwinist attitude toward both economic and social life, becoming more likely to reason that those who suffer misfortune in life deserve what they get and that others shouldn't worry too much about helping them. (In the words of one journalist, "Many people look at the ever-widening gap between rich and poor in this country and think to themselves, Hey, it's a great time to be rich.")[4]

Finally, and to a lesser extent, Americans have become somewhat more attached to status-seeking and consumption. If life is going to be a war of all against all, you might as well flaunt the spoils of your own victories, however small or great.

This may all seem a little dystopian to a reader sipping lemonade on a porch in Olympia, Washington, or half watching a Little League game in Dunlap, Illinois. Where most Americans are sitting, it probably doesn't look as though looting or *A Clockwork Orange*–style violence perpetrated by roving gangs of amoral youth are about to break out at any moment. True enough. It's important to note that these are not the *dominant* values in American society at present. But they are the values, on average, growing most rapidly. The trajectory of social change in America over the past dozen years has been away from the traditional values of both deference to authority and attraction to community (respect your elders, don't talk back, and bring over a casserole if someone from the church gets sick) and toward the more individualistic and self-centred values described above.

Most of the growth in these values is caused by intergenerational social change. It's not that individual Americans are changing their values but rather that younger Americans are simply more likely to favour the values of hard hedonism and Darwinist competition than are their parents or grandparents. And this isn't mere teenage distemper: Americans well into middle age are scoring higher on trends associated with thrill-seeking, hedonism, and Darwinism. Our data reveal deep, intergenerational values change. American teenagers aren't growing out of what we term *Exclusion and Intensity* values; American society is growing into them. As the saccharine cliché goes, children are our future—for better or for worse. The culture is shifting to a new place.

But how can it be that America's youth are leading the country toward values of hard hedonism and unscrupulous individualism even as the political climate appears to grow ever more conservative? The answer leads us back to the special character of the politically engaged that I discussed above. American voters, regardless of party preference, are becoming more attracted to values associated with order and authority. In this way engaged American citizens are steadily diverging not only from their non-voting compatriots but indeed from the net trajectory of social change in their country.

Many have attributed what they see as the increased conservatism of American politics to the trauma of 9/11, arguing that the desire for stronger leadership arises from the fear and uncertainty engendered by a sudden attack from an enemy whose motives and boundaries are equally mysterious. This may be true to some extent, but our data show that *politically engaged* Americans have had a growing attraction to authority since at least 1996. I believe the political climate in America is a reaction to the social change Americans sense is afoot at home more than a reaction to foreign enemies. Our data suggest that the "moral decline" of which religious conservatives speak with such alarm may well exist. But in their struggle to "restore America's values," many conservatives misapprehend their enemy. In terms of social change in the United States, they have much less to fear from those idealistic Deaniacs (as Howard Dean's army of energetic young supporters was nicknamed) than from their fellow Americans who don't even care to enter the discussion.

THE SOCIAL VALUES METHOD

Our method begins with a battery of over 600 questions. Our social values survey isn't a poll, but it does share some of the characteristics of polling. Like a poll, this survey asks people to do things like agree or disagree with a statement; take two ideals and prioritize one over the other; and describe their social affiliations—religious, political, demographic, and so on.

But polls usually measure one or two issues at a time; for example, what proportion of the population supports an idea or a candidate. In addition, they might cross-reference a respondent's position on an issue with his or her membership in a group, such as a political party, religious denomination, or demographic category. The social values method, by contrast, offers the analysis of multiple variables. Our statistical routines can examine not just one correlation but many at the same time. Of course, it would be impossibly confusing to try to display relationships among answers to 600 questions in a table or in writing, as polls are usually reported. Instead, we use a social values "map" that uses two-dimensional space to display relationships among many values and many people.

Take the issue of gun control. Instead of just knowing that Republicans are more likely than Democrats to favour private citizens' right to carry a concealed weapon, or that men are more likely than women to do the same, we could generate a values profile of someone who believes that any private citizen should be able to carry a concealed weapon, and gain a better sense of where that person is coming from. Is he strong on values like *Anomie-Aimlessness* and *Acceptance of Violence*, favouring concealed weapons because he's resigned to the idea that society is a war of all against all, where everyone is as disconnected, hostile, and dangerous as he is? Or is he a libertarian, strong on *Everyday Ethics* and *Civic Engagement*, who doesn't care to carry a gun himself but believes on principle that the state shouldn't be able to dictate these kinds of rules? Or is he a father, strong on *Duty* and *Patriarchy*, who believes that he must under all circumstances be able to physically overpower anyone who would threaten his family—and that a gun (which he may never fire) guarantees his ability to do so? Or is she a woman, strong on *Gender Equality* and *Personal Control*, who feels that in order to assert control over her life and person in a dangerous world, she should have the right to carry a .357 Magnum if she so desires? Values profiles allow us to link people's opinions to their overall mental postures.

THE VALUES

Before looking at the social values map, we need to understand its contents: the values we measure. Each of the values (or trends) on the map usually represents two to four actual questions[5] we've asked in our social values surveys. (A few contain just one question.) The questions are designed to measure, from different angles, a respondent's orientation to a single concept. For example, since 1992 we've been tracking a value we call *Acceptance of Violence*. This trend is made up of four items with which respondents are asked to agree or disagree on a four-point scale:

1. Violence can sometimes be exciting.
2. When a person can't take it any more and feels as if he/she is about to explode, a little violent behaviour can relieve the tension. It's no big deal.
3. Violence is a part of life. It's no big deal.
4. It's acceptable to use physical force to get something you really want. The important thing is to get what you want.

Respondents' answers on all four of these items (their degrees of agreement and disagreement) are aggregated into an overall score on the trend *Acceptance of Violence*. We ensure that the individual items that compose the trends are indeed measuring a single orientation by testing the degree to which they correlate with one another.

We make no claim that these and the other items we use are perfect measures. One of the major interpretive projects in this work is the creation of questions that effectively measure people's orientations to some meaningful concept. Survey questions, no matter how they may strive to be unbiased, are not sterile scalpels; they're made of words with all kinds of cultural baggage attached to them.

True, some surveys are intentionally biased, and their bias taints their results. When questions deliberately lead respondents in one direction to offer a misleading picture of public opinion, it's called push polling. The famous example is "If you knew that [name of political candidate] was a convicted sex offender, would you be more or less likely to vote for him?" The candidate needn't actually be a sex offender in order for the poll results (not to mention the subsequent rumours) to get pretty ugly.

One critic, in response to my last book, *Fire and Ice,* accused me of bias because some of the items in our social values survey ask people to agree or disagree with extreme, many would say offensive, views. But the goal of this survey is not to prove some absolute fact about the nature of American society. Rather, its goal is comparative: we use our data to compare groups of respondents with each other (as when we compare young with old, or New Englanders with Midwesterners) or with themselves over time. The questions we ask can be provocative, but their "bias" does not corrupt our findings, provided we keep asking people exactly the same "biased" questions. If 5 percent of American women agree with a statement widely viewed as unreasonable, and 15 percent of American men agree with the same statement, that's a worthwhile finding—no matter how unreasonable the statement might be. And if proportions agreeing or disagreeing with the statement increase or decrease over time, that too is significant.

The comparative nature of the social values method gives rise to an important difference between how we report our results and how pollsters report theirs. While polls usually show what proportion of the population agrees or disagrees with an idea, we deal primarily with relative scores on groups of questions (values) and not absolute scores on individual questions. As a result, we use index scores to express our findings.

On the value *Acceptance of Violence,* for example, we take the combined rate of agreement of the U.S. population and establish that as our base: we give it a score of 100. When we look at groups within the population (demographic groups, regional groups, political groups, and so on), their index scores show whether they're stronger or weaker on a given value than the general population. On the trend *Acceptance of Violence,* Americans under the age of twenty have an index score of 255; they're considerably more likely than average to agree with the four statements listed above. Americans over the age of sixty, by contrast, have an index score of 56; they're considerably less likely than average to agree with the four statements listed above. The social values map contains over a hundred values constructed as I've just described.

THE SOCIAL VALUES MAP

Agree or disagree: The Father of the family must be master in his own house. This is one of the most telling items in our social values survey. To some, the idea that "Father must be master" seems a self-evident truth. To others, the statement seems hopelessly outdated, or as offensive as asking whether a husband has a natural right to beat his wife. Not only do most people feel strongly about this item, but their answer—whatever it is—is so fundamental to their world view that they're often surprised to even be asked to make their position on it explicit. Does the sun revolve around the earth or vice versa? The answer is obvious and universally understood—until you run into Galileo or the Pope.

To begin to orient yourself on the map we use to display social values graphically, imagine the kind of person you think would reply "Of course!" to the statement that the father must be master of the house. Now imagine the kind of person you think would reply "You're kidding, right?" Even in the absence of data from thousands of social values surveys, you might intuit that these two imaginary souls would differ on many issues, not just the distribution of power in the family. You would probably be right. Some values on the map tend to correlate positively with each other; others correlate negatively. In other words, if we know someone believes strongly that the father must be the master of the house, we can make good predictions about the other values that person is likely to espouse.

In addition to the trend *Patriarchy*, then, let's look at three other trends located nearby on the map: *Obedience to Authority, Traditional Family,* and *Religiosity.* These values fall close together on the map because people who believe strongly in one of them are likely to believe strongly in the others as well. Americans over the age of sixty, for instance, are above the U.S. average in agreeing that the father of the family must be master of the house (we label this value *Patriarchy*). They're also above average on the trends *Traditional Family, Obedience to Authority, Duty,* and *Religiosity.*

Trends tend to hang together on the map to the extent that they hang together in people's minds; these four values frequently occur as part of a single mindset or world view.

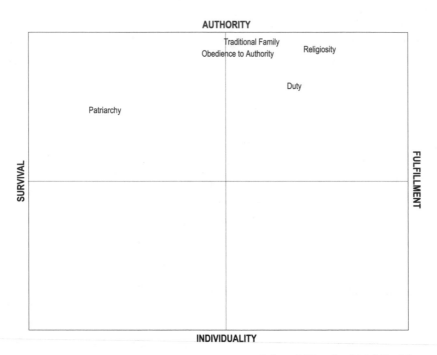

Selected Trends, 2004 Positions

The other side of this coin is that values that correlate *negatively* with each other tend to be far apart on the map. Near the bottom of the map, we find the values *Flexible Gender Identity, Penchant for Risk, Equal Relationship with Youth,* and *Sexual Permissiveness.* The fact that these values fall so far away from the ones discussed above (*Patriarchy* and so on) suggests that people who are strong on one group are likely to be weak on the other. Another look at Americans over sixty as a test case confirms this expectation: these Americans, stronger than average on *Patriarchy* and the other top-of-map values, are considerably weaker than average on many values at the bottom of the map, including *Sexual Permissiveness, Penchant for Risk, Equal Relationship with Youth,* and *Flexible Gender Identity.*

Americans over Age 60: Partial Values Profile, 2004 Data

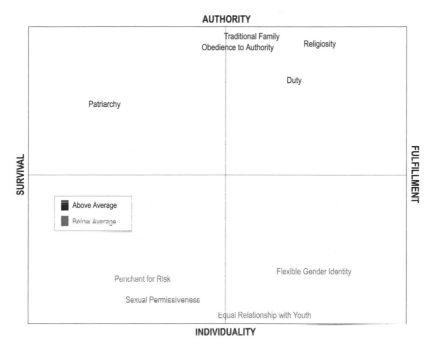

Selected Trends, 2004 Positions

When all the values are distributed in this manner, with positively correlated values close together and negatively correlated values far apart, discrete and coherent mental postures begin to emerge in different areas of the map.

The U.S. values map is defined by two axes.[6] The vertical axis positions values that are oriented toward Authority at the top of the map and values oriented toward Individuality at the bottom of the map. The horizontal axis positions values associated with personal Fulfillment at the right of the map and values associated with sheer Survival at the left of the map. The two axes yield four quadrants, which we've labelled (on the next page) according to the values they contain. Each quadrant's label points to the world view that emerges when all the values in that quadrant are considered together.

AUTHORITY

Status & Security:
Obedience to Traditional Structures and Norms

Authenticity & Responsibility:
Well-being, Harmony, and Responsibility

SURVIVAL

FULFILLMENT

Exclusion & Intensity:
Seeking Stimulus and Attention

Idealism & Autonomy:
Exploration and Flexibility

INDIVIDUALITY

Plotting People on the Map

Once the parameters of the map are established and all the values are in place, we're able to plot individuals and groups in the map space just as we plot values. The place that a person or group occupies on the map is determined by the values they embrace or reject most strongly. A group's position on the map is the average position of all the individual respondents within that group.

We've just seen that Americans over the age of sixty are stronger than average on some top-of-map values and weaker than average on some of those at the bottom. When their scores on all the trends are taken into account and the computer plots them, the result is fairly intuitive. Americans over age sixty fall near the top of the map, close to the authority-oriented values they embrace most strongly.

Recall the two imaginary people you recently conjured—the ones who agreed and disagreed, respectively, with the idea that the father of the family must be master of the house. Perhaps these imaginary respondents took the form of the stereotypical Red and Blue Americans, one registering

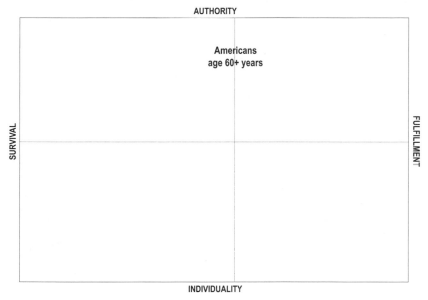

AUTHORITY

Americans
age 60+ years

SURVIVAL

FULFILLMENT

INDIVIDUALITY

2004 Data

his belief that Dad should be boss from in front of his gun rack equipped pickup (conservative talk radio audible through the window), the other glancing up wearily from her latte and laptop in a San Francisco café.

If we ask the computer to plot those two people on the map based on their responses to that one question *only*, the person who agreed that Father must be master would fall right on top of the trend Patriarchy in the upper-left *(Status and Security)* quadrant of the map, and the person who disagreed would be in roughly the opposite area of the map: the lower-right *(Idealism and Autonomy)* quadrant.

But the map contains, as we've begun to see, not just this one value, but more than a hundred values relating to all aspects of life: religion, the family, the environment, consumption, self-image, social belonging, justice, violence, community, gender, health … the list goes on.

The positions of our two hypothetical respondents might change considerably depending on their values in these other areas. The person who disagrees with "Father must be master" might do so on grounds of sheer egalitarianism, falling into the *Authenticity and Responsibility* quadrant near the value *Gender Parity*. This person might simply

AUTHORITY

**Strong
Patriarchy**

SURVIVAL

FULFILLMENT

**Weak
Patriarchy**

INDIVIDUALITY

2004 Data

believe that women and men are inherently equal and that God made
them that way.

Another way to disagree with the "Father must be master" statement is
on the grounds that men and women aren't just equal but are social
constructs with *no* inherent properties other than anatomical ones. This
person might be in the lower-right *Idealism and Autonomy* quadrant near
the trend *Flexible Gender Identity*.

A third person might disagree that Father should be master because he
or she rejects all forms of hierarchy, and even all forms of social order. This
person would fall into the *Exclusion and Intensity* quadrant, strong on
values like *Anomie-Aimlessness* and *Civic Apathy*. Each quadrant of our
map, with it's full slate of values, is displayed in Appendix C.

TALK ABOUT "VALUES"—particularly in the political sphere—is too
often limited to a narrow set of binaries on such issues as abortion, guns,
same-sex marriage, the death penalty, prayer in schools, and so on: those

now famous "moral values." The social values map offers a broader terrain in which we can think about and discuss values; it offers an empirical basis for dispassionate discussions of values (I am an optimist) and how they are changing; and, crucially, it allows us to examine correlations among a diverse set of values—analysis that yields not two possible ways of seeing the world but a set of possibilities that's almost boundless. With this tool, the shopworn stereotypes of the gun rack and the latte can be, if not eliminated, then assigned their rightful (marginal) place in discussions of American social values and social change.

one

Retrenchment and Renewal

Excess and vulgarity, as always, enjoy a vast, bipartisan constituency,
and in a democracy no political party will ever stamp them out.
—Frank Rich

Iɴ ᴛʜᴇ ᴜɴɪᴛᴇᴅ sᴛᴀᴛᴇs there's such a thing as a South Park Conservative. To those familiar with the animated comedy *South Park,* this will perhaps come as a surprise. The show is consistently and deliberately outrageous, leaving no taboo—racial, sexual, religious, or political—unprobed. Some of its more famous moments include the introduction of "Mr. Hanky, the Christmas Poo," a piece of excrement in a tiny Santa hat who teaches an eight-year-old Jewish character about the spirit of Christmas; a town "whore-off" in which competitors demonstrate their abilities by inserting ever larger and more ungainly items (and ultimately their opponents) into their nether orifices; and a special episode in the week following Terri Schiavo's death in which one of the characters lobbies to have his vegetative friend's feeding tube removed in order that he might inherit the injured boy's PSP video game player.

South Park seems to be the kind of program that conservatives would trot out as exemplary of America's toxic popular culture—shocking, depraved, and obscene. The show has certainly drawn plenty of criticism (the whore-off, to choose just one example, was featured as one of the Parents Television Council's most offensive TV scenes of the week). But some Republicans revel in the show's contempt for the political correctness they see as being enforced by that favourite cabal, the "liberal elite." Republican pundit Brian C. Anderson has written a book on conservative responses to American media and sees South Park Conservatives as such a telling group that he named his book after them.

South Park Conservatives are interesting because they reside at the juncture of two great and seemingly opposing forces in American public life: a political landscape that has become significantly more conservative and moralistic, and an entertainment culture that seems to know no restraint.

What are we to make of these two faces of America that, in their way, articulate the classic American struggle between collective moralism and individual licence? Are the armies of the "culture war" real—with red moralists on one side and blue hedonists on the other, and blue-dominated Hollywood inflicting its idea of entertainment on a populace half-titillated and half-horrified? Or do the same people in fact hunger for both *Grand Theft Auto* and Bush-style moral values, as in Churchill County, Nevada, where 71 percent of voters supported a second term for a teetotalling, born-again president in 2004 and where at the same time 63 percent voted to keep the county's brothels legal?

There are, of course, ideological responses to these questions. Karl Rove, in explaining the 2004 Republican victory on *Meet the Press,* described the moral-values crowd thus: "I think it's people who are concerned about the coarseness of our culture, about what they see on the television sets, what they see in the movies, what they read in the newspapers, how they see the values of the country, what they see as the future for our country." This view positions moral-values voters as fighting a noble and weary battle against the smut peddlers who would corrupt their children. Meanwhile, some Democrats claim that the culture war is fuelled to a great extent by hypocrisy: Republicans like a Desperate Housewife as much as anyone—they just don't like to admit it. (Laura Bush jokingly conceded as much in a speech at the annual White House Correspondents' Association dinner; poking fun at her husband's early-to-bed habits, the first lady remarked, "Nine o'clock, Mr. Excitement here is sound asleep and I'm watching *Desperate*

*"How about one more round of 'God Bless America'
before we bring out the naked broads."*

Housewives with Lynne Cheney. Ladies and gentlemen, I am a desperate housewife.")

The hypocrisy goes beyond mere entertainment consumption, these Democrats argue, given that "sin" rates (divorce, crime, out-of-wedlock births) are higher in red states than in blue states.[1] So for Republicans to parade about as the guardians of propriety while casting stones at liberals seems to Democrats both laughable and unjust.

But as America's politicians wrangle about which side of the aisle is to blame for the country's social ills and the entertainment that represents, magnifies, and glorifies perfidy, both sides miss a crucial fact. The battle between traditional ideals of morality and propriety and the sometimes outrageous results of America's tradition of individual licence is *not* a partisan battle. What many Republicans, and also many Democrats, fail to see is that it's not primarily Democrats or Democratic values the cultural conservatives are fighting against.[2] The social trends that conservatives find most dismaying are being driven by a large segment of the population—the plurality, in fact—whose values are not expressed by any political party.

In short, the current political landscape of the United States belies the trajectory of the country's social change. While American politics becomes increasingly committed to a brand of conservatism that favours traditionalism, religiosity, and authority, our values data show the culture at large becoming ever more attached to hedonism, thrill-seeking, and a ruthless, Darwinist understanding of human competition.

To situate this evolution on the social values map we explored in the introduction, American culture at large is moving down and left, into the *Exclusion and Intensity* quadrant. That is, Americans on average are moving away from both the moralism and deference to authority at the top of the map and the communitarianism and fulfillment orientation at the right of the map.

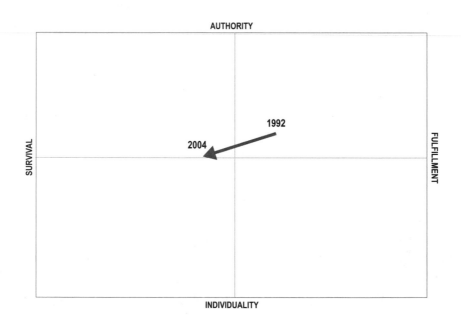

WHAT'S DRIVING AMERICA'S MOVEMENT ON THE MAP?

The mindset distilled in the lower-left quadrant rejects both authority and deep fulfillment as foundations of meaning and right conduct. In other words, it does not grant other people (authority figures such as parents, employers, or religious leaders) or abstractions (God, codes of propriety, hierarchies of respect, as in "respect your elders") the power to dictate what it should and should not do, as those at the top of the map do. Nor does it seek to construct its own rules about right and wrong through deep introspection, as those at the right of the map do, asking such questions as "Should I treat others as I would like to be treated?" "What would happen if everyone acted the way I do?" "What sort of world is just and happy, and how would individuals in that world behave?" and "What are my responsibilities to others, and what effect does it have on my own well-being when I fail to live up to them?"

This is not to say that those whose values place them in the lower-left quadrant necessarily break the law, or fail to hold jobs, or harm others at every opportunity. Indeed, crime rates have actually fallen during the period our surveys measure, so we know these changes in values haven't translated into a growth in reported legal transgressions. But it's important to note that in the world view of the lower-left quadrant, the constraints that keep people from transgressing society's rules, whether its laws or its informal rules of etiquette, are much fewer than the rules and norms that keep people in other areas of the map in line.

Those at the top of the map follow rules because they fear retribution from God or man: eternal damnation, legal punishment, or a good swat from Dad. In an orthodox version of this world view, the punishments of family, state, and God are interlinked: Dad has to punish his son to keep him out of trouble with the law, and ultimately out of hell. In his famous *Life of Johnson,* James Boswell recounts the words of a highly punitive Latin teacher of Samuel Johnson's. He would beat his students severely while repeating soberly, "And this I do to save you from the gallows." (Johnson approved of this pedagogical approach; when asked how he'd become such an accomplished student of Latin, he replied, "My master whipt me very well. Without that, Sir, I should have done nothing.")

Those at the right of the map follow rules because they've internalized the reasons for the rules: they empathize with others and so don't want to harm them, whether through reckless driving or social insults. The golden rule, do unto others as you would have them do unto you, evokes the idea that rules of good conduct can be derived from introspection and empathy[3]—knowing one's own needs and feelings and attempting to empathize with the needs and feelings of others.

Of course, both of these "rule-following" types are distilled: most people have lots of reasons for following their society's rules, some of which derive from fear of reprimand and some of which come from an internalized, emotional aversion to anti-social behaviour. As the map displaying America's values trajectory shows, Americans have in the past been located in the upper-right quadrant, where exactly this combination of values would have been at work in keeping people polite, law-abiding, and helpful. But those values are being eroded in America; while people may not be breaking more *laws*,[4] many Americans have noted a general decline in adherence to less formal rules in society, rules of etiquette and courtesy.

In his book *Bowling Alone,* political scientist Robert Putnam explores what he calls America's declining "social capital" by charting the erosion of good social manners among Americans in the latter half of the twentieth century. Putnam argues that a subtle but measurable disregard for others is becoming more pervasive in America, a change he attributes to diminished trust among strangers. In 1952 a slim majority of Americans believed that people in general were as "honest and moral" as they used to be; by 1998 only half that proportion, just over a quarter of Americans, said the same. If people aren't to be trusted, then they don't deserve much courtesy; Putnam writes that people under the age of forty-five are twice as likely as those over forty-five to screen calls. Behaviour on the roads is equally indifferent. In 1953 a quarter of Americans reported that they'd driven over eighty-five miles per hour. By 1992 the proportion had risen to nearly half (49 percent). Failure to observe stop signs has also increased hugely, as has Americans' sense that "people" are becoming more reckless on the roads (three-quarters of Americans in

1997 said that people were driving more aggressively than five years before). It all adds up to an atmosphere of suspicion of and indifference toward others. The ratio of Americans who say "most people can be trusted" to those who say "you can't be too careful in dealing with people" has been tilting toward distrust since 1960, and as of the late 1990s, only about a third of adults and a quarter of teenagers reported that they felt they could trust their fellow citizens.

Little wonder that Putnam notes this atmosphere of diminished trust and ergo courtesy (and vice versa—it's a vicious cycle); the move into the lower-left quadrant of the values map would suggest nothing else. Because the world view expressed in the lower-left quadrant rejects both authority (top of map) and fulfillment (right of map) as pillars to structure one's behaviour and one's pursuit of desired ends, this world view tends to be preoccupied with immediacy: immediate gratification, self-interest as defined here and now, pleasure as an unexamined, visceral experience, and status signified by ostentatious displays of material symbols of success. Whereas the values of both authority and fulfillment focus on the longer term—the cultivation of a good character, the accumulation of respect from others over time, the pursuit of God's favour—the lower-left quadrant wants what it wants when it wants it; deferred gratification is for suckers.

As a result of this insistence on immediacy, the lower-left quadrant is generally defined by values that fall into three broad categories: intensity and thrill-seeking, Darwinism and exclusion, and consumption and status-seeking. In the period from 1992 to 2004, American society's movement into the lower-left quadrant was driven by the average American's growing attachment to values associated with intensity and thrill-seeking, and Darwinism and exclusion. Trends related to consumption, by contrast, have remained fairly stable. Here again it bears noting that these observations relate to how Americans' values are *changing*, not which values define America. It's not that consumption is unimportant in America, but its importance is remaining fairly constant, as it has on a mass scale since the 1950s. Similarly, the values that our surveys indicate are in decline, which range from *National Pride* to *Introspection and*

Empathy, are far from irrelevant, but they're in decline relative to many of the values in the *Exclusion and Intensity* quadrant that this chapter will describe.

Intensity and Thrill-Seeking

The popular 1999 movie *Fight Club* begins with one man's dissatisfaction with his banal life, which he lives surrounded by Ikea furniture and grey, office-cubicle walls. His existence makes him feel numb and emasculated. The arc of the story begins in earnest when he experiences the thrill of being beaten to a pulp in a midnight parking lot; the sensation is painful but it's strong—and strong, he decides, even if it's bad, is good. Over time, his pleasure in intensity becomes a nationwide movement. It turns out that men all over America—living as they do in a child-proofed, politically correct, safe-sexed, dumbed-down, media-addicted society—are longing for the same raw sensations: punches given and taken, fights won and lost, intense, physical, manly feelings. Strong is good. Real is better.

In reflecting on Americans' desire for strong leadership after 9/11, Bill Clinton remarked, "When people feel uncertain, they would rather have somebody who is wrong and strong than somebody who is right and weak." At this cultural and historical moment, Americans seem to be preoccupied with strength, in its connotations of both power (the might, resolve, and resilience of a person or a state) and intensity (the extent to which an experience can utterly absorb a person, in excitement, or pleasure, or even fear, however briefly). If the desire for strong political leadership is driven by uncertainty about national security, it may be that the desire for strong experiences is propelled by an uncertainty about more existential matters. In this view, George W. Bush and his seeming opposites in the realms of hedonism and thrill-seeking are responses to different facets of the same condition of insecurity about how one can stay authentic, safe, happy, and good all at once in contemporary America.

Between 1992 and 2004, Americans on average had increasingly high scores on a number of trends associated with intensity and thrill-seeking.

The trend *Pursuit of Intensity,* on which Americans' average score increased, measures respondents' desire to seek out intense experiences as well as to act more according to impulses and emotions than to rational considerations.

Americans also grew stronger on *Attraction for Crowds,* indicating a growing desire to share experiences like concerts and other public events with large assemblies of people. Here I am reminded, paradoxically, of the American migration to suburbs and then outer suburbs (or exurbs): the quest for a sense of space and freedom in residential areas of ever lower density, the migratory articulation of Sartre's existential dictum that hell is other people. Even as they seek to escape other people and their attendant problems (noise, crime, traffic, lineups, rudeness), Americans still long for connectedness.

As people become lonelier, their atavistic craving for emotional exchange grows. The farther Americans move from each other, within their sprawling communities and even inside their increasingly gargantuan homes, the more they long for the feelings that can only come from social contact. Hence the stadium and the megachurch, the temples of Americans' collective secular and religious life. (The evangelical men's group the Promise Keepers, launched by a football coach, even combines the religious and the secular to achieve a single pumped-up crowd experience: men collectively worship, hug, and pledge to keep their promises, all usually in the reassuringly macho setting of a sports stadium.) It is mere coincidence but fitting that perhaps the three largest communal experiences in America—Thanksgiving, Christmas, and the Super Bowl—all occur as winter descends and the elements impose even greater isolation upon the nation that once turned its lonely eyes to Joltin' Joe DiMaggio.

The evangelical megachurch is a relatively recent shift in congregational organization. In 1970 there were ten such megachurches (those with 2,000 members or more) in the United States; in 2005, there are 282. Church attendance in the United States has stayed fairly constant since the 1950s—about four in ten Americans report going to church weekly—so megachurches aren't a result of Americans' flocking to churches as never before. But the rise of the megachurch does signal a crucial shift in the *form* of American religious practice. Some observers of U.S. social trends have remarked that megachurches, with their cafés, gyms, daycare centres, counselling services, and other resources, offer a ready community gathering place, complete with some vital social services the American government does not offer its citizens. I agree that these are important factors in the growth of megachurches. But a neglected draw of these massive organizations, I believe, is the sheer ecstatic thrill of worship services—with rock bands, plasma-screen displays accompanying live performances (musical, dramatic, and rhetorical), and hundreds upon hundreds of fellow singers, prayers, worshippers, shouters, and spectators.

In July 2005 the Lakewood Church held its first service in the Compaq Center, the former arena of the Houston Rockets. There was not a seat to spare in the stadium-cum-church, which has a capacity of 16,000 (a "Texas-sized sanctuary," in the words of its pastor, Joel Osteen).[5] The special intensity that comes from being part of a large crowd of people is one that Americans are increasingly craving. Many are seeking this intensity at concerts and other public entertainment events, but a growing number of Americans are choosing to experience their weekly religious services with a side serving of this crowd-induced thrill (or vice versa). Tellingly, the Lakewood Church's first service was held not on a bright and sober Sunday morning but on Saturday night: party night.

Another value whose importance grew for Americans in the 1992 to 2004 period was *Intuition and Impulse*. This change points to a greater openness among Americans to pay attention to—and even allow their opinions and decisions to be guided by—gut feelings and mood changes. Perhaps anticipating Malcolm Gladwell's spirited defence of first impressions in his most recent book, *Blink,* a growing proportion of Americans report being interested in their personal intuition and often willing to go with their instincts. Gladwell's book isn't about intuition in any shadowy or extrasensory way; it's about the rapid processing of information our brains do in the split second when they're asked to evaluate something.

Whether they've read Gladwell's defence of the first impression or not, Americans increasingly report that they buy it.

Americans during this period also grew stronger on the trend *Penchant for Risk*. This value measures respondents' willingness to take risks both to achieve goals and for the sake of the risky experience itself. I'd like to examine the value *Penchant for Risk* and see how it's contributing to Americans' movement on the map.

Americans are often seen—and often see themselves—as a risk-taking people, from the earliest settlers who sailed across the Atlantic toward an unknown continent to those who risked their lives to immigrate (legally or otherwise) just last year and those who stake their savings on a business venture or their reputations on a scientific innovation. Risk, like apple pie, is part of America.

But the trend *Penchant for Risk* is an exaggeration of the kind of risk that underpins the classic story of American striving. This trend often implies an understanding of risk not as a means of achieving something of great value but as an end in itself. *Penchant for Risk* includes two items: one that sees risk instrumentally, as a way to "get what I want," and another that sees risk simply as an exhilarating experience. The first item garners higher rates of agreement, but the two correlate strongly, and both tend to be most eagerly embraced by those whose values are not governed by a sense of purpose beyond their own immediate sensations and desires—whether that greater purpose be religious, moral, communitarian, or personal.

Penchant for Risk

	1992	1996	2000	2004
In order to get what I want, I would be prepared to take great risks in life.	26	28	38	41
From time to time I like to do things that are dangerous or forbidden just for the sake of the risk and the sensation.	18	19	31	32

Percentage agreeing

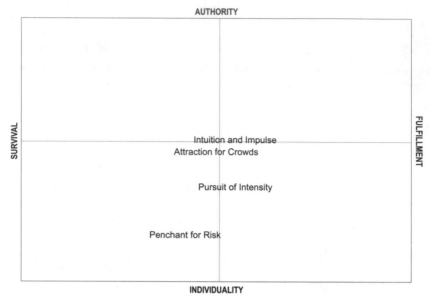

AUTHORITY

SURVIVAL

FULFILLMENT

Intuition and Impulse
Attraction for Crowds

Pursuit of Intensity

Penchant for Risk

INDIVIDUALITY

Thrill-Seeking Trends, 2004 Positions

Darwinism and Exclusion

Thrills and risk for their own sake define a portion of the emerging mental posture in America, but there's more. A second pull factor drawing that mythic average American into the lower-left quadrant of the map is the increasing attraction to values associated with Darwinism and exclusion. Of course, by Darwinism I don't mean an actual surge in support for eugenics or other abandoned social engineering schemes, but rather a mindset that sees brutal competition as a natural, exhilarating, and even cleansing condition for human coexistence.

Most of the values I call "Darwinist" are found along the extreme left edge of the social values map: trends such as *Acceptance of Violence* and *Just Deserts* indicate a dog-eat-dog world view in which winners win by any means necessary, including violence, and losers get what they deserve—and are unworthy of sympathy or help.[6] Values like *Sexism* and *Xenophobia* indicate a belief that some inequality is inherent, not an injustice to be repaired, and that people should act according to their own self-interest without worrying about negative consequences for other lesser beings.

Some kinds of competition, like some kinds of risk-taking, are simply part of America—and indeed part of the way most living organisms and successful societies seem to seek out scarce resources. But societies usually temper the law of the jungle, the Hobbesian war of all against all, by attempting to transform it into the most productive and least damaging version of itself. America has long prized competition, and free individuals in its free market have been spurred to wonderful achievements. But America has also long prized fairness. It is this dedication to fairness that led America to adopt a system of universal public education so early: its leaders aimed to get everyone to the same starting line so that when the starter pistol sounded, the race would be fair and the winner would be deserving. The vision of competition apparent in values like *Acceptance of Violence,* however, does not unfold in a structure designed with fairness in mind: it's a no-holds-barred, might-makes-right competition.

I read *Sexism* and *Xenophobia* as Darwinist trends because they differ fundamentally from the approach that says "Here's the starting line and here are the rules; may the best and hardest-working among us win." Rather, they suggest that some people are inherently inferior and don't deserve a fair shake. If they weren't lucky enough to be born white, male, and American, too bad. It doesn't matter if the competition isn't fair, and it doesn't matter if some are barred from entry. Those who survive and prosper are *by definition* the most worthy.

Many people expected an upsurge of xenophobic sentiment in the United States in the wake of 9/11. But in fact, overall growth in the value *Xenophobia* was sharper from 1992 to 2000—when the U.S. economy and stock market were on the up and when most Americans were happy to have Bill Clinton as their president—than from 2000 to 2004. In 1992 we asked Americans to agree or disagree with the statement "Non-whites should not be allowed to immigrate to our country"; 16 percent of Americans agreed. By the year 2000, that proportion had risen to 25 percent. But the trend remained flat between 2000 and 2004. Similarly, when asked to agree or disagree that "Overall, there is too much immigration.

It threatens the purity of our country," half of Americans agreed in 2004. Perhaps that number seems surprisingly high, but the same proportion of Americans agreed with the statement in 1996. In other words, 9/11 did not increase American xenophobia.

Sexism is also surprisingly strong in America these days. In a nation that cultural conservatives claim has been utterly overtaken by feminism (or femi-Nazism, in one of Rush Limbaugh's more outrageous coinages), 35 percent still believe that "men have a certain natural superiority over women and nothing can change this." The proportion agreeing with this statement has risen by 4 percent since 1992. Condoleezza Rice may be secretary of state, but for a third of Americans Condi's position can be explained by her exceptional status (she's a member of the weaker sex who has transcended her natural limitations), political correctness (to which the Bush administration uncharacteristically conceded her appointment), or both.

In addition to growing indifference to social inequality, we find the value *Ecological Fatalism* to be on the rise, pointing to an increasing sense that environmental destruction is unavoidable—another rationale for the pursuit of individuals' narrowly defined interests without regard for such irrelevant externalities as ecological damage or social inequality. It's another puzzle piece in a zero-sum world view; in this case not me versus you, men versus women, or American versus outsider, but "the economy" versus "the environment."

Rejecting the belief that these two ideas—economy and environment—aren't mutually exclusive and can't be sustainably pitted against each other, the lower-left quadrant takes the attitude that there has to be a winner and a loser: if people are strong enough and smart enough to squeeze what they want from the earth, it's their right to do so. That's called winning (for now). If an individual has money to burn—in the form of gas for the Hummer, heating for a home that's three times as large as necessary, cars for every member of the family so no one must suffer the indignity of walking, taking public transit, or carpooling— then he should do so; these are the spoils of his economic victories and they are his right.

Darwinist Trends, 2004 Positions

Reality television is full of the winner take all Darwinism we find on the map: the chosen Apprentice or Survivor gets all the spoils, regardless of how he or she has played the game. Might (and/or manipulation, deceit, betrayal, and so on) makes right. In *The Apprentice,* real estate mogul Donald Trump selects his next hire (and ostensible protégé) from a pack of young, ruthless hopefuls. In other words, the patriarch (complete with ostentatious golden crown, combed over majestically) hand-picks the winner. In the *Survivor* model, the winner is decided according to the tyranny of the majority. In neither case is there any compromise, cooperation, or conciliation (unless you count conspiracy under one of these headings), and the dispatch of losers is a spectacle of rejection.

One of the most telling trends in this Darwinist zone on the map is *Acceptance of Violence.* As I did with *Penchant for Risk,* I'd like to analyze *Acceptance of Violence* here, describing the individual questions it comprises and how Americans' responses are changing over time.

Acceptance of Violence was the single fastest-growing value in America from 1992 to 2004. Other values remain more important in defining the

American mindset in absolute terms, but in terms of *change* over the past twelve years, *Acceptance of Violence* is a crucial part of the story. This change is an attitudinal one; I'm not arguing that violence is sweeping America. (As I noted above, official crime rates are in decline.) But the way many Americans are *thinking about* violence appears to be changing in an important way. The trend *Acceptance of Violence* measures the extent to which respondents believe that violence is an inevitable part of life, cathartic for its perpetrator and persuasive for its victim. A high score on *Acceptance of Violence* suggests that the respondent has no special aversion to violence as a strategy and assigns it no special moral import, but rather sees it as one of several ways of approaching a problem.

Acceptance of Violence is the aggregate of four items with which respondents are asked to agree or disagree on a four-point scale. The rates of agreement with each of these items over the four waves of our survey are shown in the table below:

Acceptance of Violence

	1992	1996	2000	2004
When a person can't take it any more and feels as if he/she is about to explode, a little violent behaviour can relieve the tension. It's no big deal.	15	27	31	32
Violence can sometimes be exciting.	23	23	27	25
Violence is a part of life. It's no big deal.	10	18	24	20
It's acceptable to use physical force to get something you really want. The important thing is to get what you want.	9	17	24	23

Percentage agreeing

The proportions agreeing with each of these statements remain minorities. But the rates of agreement with three of the four items that constitute *Acceptance of Violence* have *at least* doubled over the past twelve years. Moreover, the numbers shown in the table above represent the responses of the entire population, including older Americans and women, both of whom have lower rates of agreement. I'll describe demographic distinctions in greater detail later, but for now it bears noting that as of 2004, the proportion of people over age sixty agreeing with the item beginning "It's acceptable to use physical force to get something you really want" is 14 percent. Among American teenagers (aged fifteen to twenty), the rate of agreement is nearly four in ten (38 percent).

Some would argue that increased *Acceptance of Violence* is not at odds with growing political conservatism. After all, it's the Republican Party that's more fervently attached to gun rights for individuals; it's the Republican Party that has resolved to "take the fight to the enemy" in the war on terror, prizing pre-emptive violence abroad over mere vigilance at home; and it's the Republican Party that's more vocal in its support for violent retribution for murderers (the death penalty) Consequently, it's a plausible claim that the Republican Party is the party more comfortable with the exercise of violence—and that growth in the trend *Acceptance of Violence* is consistent with a shift to the right in the political landscape.

But the trend *Acceptance of Violence* has relatively little to do with these ideological orientations to violence. Instead it tends to correlate more with Darwinist trends—those associated with a ruthless, utterly self-interested world view, not one that seeks to protect cherished rights or principles through the strategic use of violence. Indeed, politically engaged Americans of both parties score well below average on *Acceptance of Violence*. Growth in this trend is driven by the young and the politically disengaged—not by Charlton Heston's loyal troops.

CONSUMPTION AND STATUS-SEEKING

Americans are famous for their consumption. Buying stuff is part of the American lifestyle, but also part of the American identity. The American Dream, although it's a package stuffed with longings, is at bottom a material dream: being better off tomorrow than today; kids being more comfortable than their parents. Sure, that perfect home of the Dream is assumed to contain a perfectly harmonious nuclear family and be surrounded by perfect neighbours, but the home itself is the focal point.

When President Bush, in the wake of 9/11, told Americans that they could make a civic contribution by shopping, some cringed. After such an immense collective trauma, weren't family and spirituality and great political questions the priorities of the day? Hadn't the quotidian getting and spending of September 10 been swept aside by a nation-shaking event? On one level, shopping seemed a trivial response to a momentous horror. On another, what the president was asking of his fellow citizens (beyond their help in buoying a rattled economy) was to keep being Americans. American people aren't *merely* shoppers, of course, but consumption, commerce, and material striving are deeply embedded in the American character. As President Calvin Coolidge famously said, "The chief business of the American people is business." And business means consumers.

Because of its deeply held meritocratic ideal, the equation between wealth and admirable personal characteristics (hard work, intelligence, discipline, resourcefulness) is perhaps more strongly felt in America than anywhere else. The kind and quality of a person's possessions, then, says almost everything about his or her worth—moral and net.

In the last section we looked at values that prize fierce (what I call Darwinist) competition: competition that is, at least metaphorically, about the struggle for survival. Just left of centre on the values map, we find values associated with competition of a different kind: the competition for attention and esteem. Trends such as *Ostentatious Consumption, Crude Materialism,* and *Need for Status Recognition* point to a desire for social status as expressed by material possessions. *Joy of Consumption* and *Buying on Impulse* point to taking visceral pleasure in the act of consumption, while *Advertising as Stimulus* measures the pleasure respondents derive from commercial advertising and the extent to which they welcome it as an invitation to consume. All these trends hover in or around the lower-left quadrant of the map, with its individualistic and status-seeking world view.

It's worth noting that these consumption-oriented values cluster closer to the centre of the map, while the more hostile, Darwinist trends cluster along its extreme left edge. Those whose values would place them among the consumption cluster are sufficiently engaged with their society to wish to signify their success to others and thus acquire social status. Those at the extreme left of the map, by contrast, are so intent on Survival values that it's winning *against* others—not merely gaining their esteem—that becomes the most important priority. Neither group is sufficiently fulfillment-oriented to judge themselves primarily according to personal standards of well-being and quality of life, but the consumers in the middle-left zone are less hard-edged than the competitors in the far-left zone.

Consumption trends were somewhat inconsistent in the 1992 to 2004 period. Americans do not report being much more likely to make impulse purchases or to take pleasure from the mere act of spending money. When it comes to the cultural meaning of their purchases, however, Americans have become somewhat more likely to say that they try to impress others with their homes and possessions. They also register increasing confidence in advertising, believing that widely advertised products are more likely to be of good quality.

A fascinating pop cultural development of the past several years has been the makeover sub-genre of reality television. The makeover is an American tradition: part of the promise of America is the promise of starting over—coming to its shores, anglicizing your name, moving west, moving to the Big Apple, a new job, a new life, a new face, and a new me. One could even say that America itself is an extreme makeover (of Europe).

The show *Extreme Makeover,* whose contestants alter their very bodies through surgery, is no doubt the most radical of the genre. But MTV's *Pimp My Ride* is my favourite. Each episode of *Pimp My Ride* selects a lucky car owner (lemon owner would be more accurate) whose miserable vehicle will be overhauled to maximum bling effect by the auto-artistes of West Coast Customs. The cars invariably receive major power injections and sleek paint jobs, but the customization is where the real fun starts: from bamboo floors to brain-blowing stereos to hot tubs and pool tables.

Cars are most people's biggest assets other than their homes. And while only a fraction of the people we know will ever know what our home looks like (the home makeover shows focus much more heavily on family harmony than on social acceptability), thousands of people will spot us in our car. Its make and model has tremendous symbolic resonance. When Japanese cars began to rival the big Detroit automakers, one used to be able to spot the odd American car with an extremely hostile—even racist—slogan denouncing Japanese makes. For these drivers the car was obviously not just a car, it was a patriotic statement; and by the same calculus, a Toyota was treason. Of course, globalization has eroded the outright xenophobia that was once aimed at some foreign imports (many of which are now, like Bruce Springsteen, born in the U.S.A.), but it remains true that our cars—from ostentatious gas guzzlers to the equally ostentatious hydrogen (and/or electricity) sippers—announce plenty more about us than that we need to get from A to B.

What makes *Pimp My Ride* so much fun (other than its sheer excess and the creativity of the car doctors) is that the episodes begin with people who are fed up with—and, crucially, *embarrassed by*—their awful cars. They don't feel their cars represent them well in a culture where your car is supposed to be an expression of your identity. By the end of the show, the car has been transformed not only into a luxury object (no matter its original make—one Honda Civic was given gull-wing doors that pivot upward instead of outward, like the doors on a DeLorean) but into one of the most highly customized vehicles on the road. It's gone from being cheap and anonymous to expensive and tremendously individual. And in a delicious development on the other side of the Atlantic, MTV is demonstrating great cultural sensitivity in expanding the Pimp franchise: Germany has aired one season of *Pimp My Bike,* and word has it that *Pimp My Scooter* is in the works.

While *Pimp My Ride* may not express the very soul of America, it's interesting that the fun of the show derives from taking an existing vehicle and making it work better both as a car and as a symbol. It would be much cheaper and easier just to ditch the lemon and buy a new car—even a very expensive one. But it's not the buying that counts. To paraphrase Bill Clinton's buddy James Carville, it's the meaning, stupid.

Another important shift in consumption-related values over the 1992–2004 period occurs in the trend we label *Saving on Principle*. Not only is this a fascinating trend, but it's also one that reveals an important phenomenon in values research: sometimes we can measure something important without initially understanding exactly what we're measuring.

We conceived of the value *Saving on Principle* in order to capture an abstemious, traditional approach to personal finances as expressed in the adage "A penny saved is a penny earned." Respondents were asked to weigh two sets of options: "Which of these two opinions about money do you hold? Money is for saving versus money is for spending"; and "If you had children, would you most want to teach them … to save and conserve their money or to spend wisely and choose their purchases carefully?"

Look how both items have been changing over time (unfortunately, we created this trend only in 1996 and so don't have 1992 data):

	1996	2000	2004
Money is for saving.	48	50	54
Money is for spending.	51	49	45
Children should be taught to save and conserve their money.	28	39	40
Children should be taught to spend wisely and choose their purchases carefully.	72	59	59

Percentage choosing option stated

On the surface, change in this value suggests that Americans are increasingly intent on saving their money. The data on consumer debt, however, suggest this is not the case. Remarkably, we've discovered over time that the people who are most likely to offer the most savings-oriented responses to these questions ("money is for saving," and "children should be taught to save and conserve their money") tend to have high scores on many of our more consumption-oriented trends. They also tend to feel greater anxiety about their personal financial circumstances. So the rising *Saving on Principle* scores are essentially a guilt response: although Americans aren't expressing greater enthusiasm for consumption, they are expressing greater anxiety about their spending. This anxiety is manifested in their *aspirational* claims about the importance they place on saving money. (We may need to invent a new value such as *Aspirational Frugality* as we track this phenomenon. Stay tuned.)

Consumption Trends, 2004 Positions

Overall, then, the pull forces that are drawing Americans into the lower-left quadrant are the growing attraction to values associated with exclusion and cutthroat competition, thrill-seeking and risk-taking (for fun and profit), and, to a lesser extent, symbolically resonant consumption. But the story of American social change doesn't end there.

WHAT ABOUT MORAL VALUES?

That Americans are moving increasingly toward values governed by the amoral pursuit of pleasure and narrowly defined self-interest is certainly counterintuitive given the current American political landscape. Aren't "moral values" the ascendant force in U.S. politics? Hasn't "liberalism" become un-American, let alone wanton hedonism? Aren't evangelical megachurches moving into sports arenas in order to seat their huge and rapidly growing flocks who thirst for strict rules about what's right and wrong, good and evil?

That's the way many outsiders see America these days, and it's the way many Americans see their compatriots: a plurality of Americans believe that politics in the United States has become more conservative in the past ten years. In an Economist/YouGov poll conducted in February 2005, 42 percent of Americans said they believed the country's politics had gotten more conservative in the previous decade, compared with 31 percent who thought politics were more liberal and 15 percent who said the political spectrum had remained about the same.

Our data suggest that the supposed groundswell of conservatism—and particularly traditionalism—among ordinary Americans has been much overstated. It's certainly not that most Americans are ardent progressives who would support a European-style Green party if given the chance, and there is little doubt that Republicans have done a better job than Democrats have of appealing to voters over the last several years. But to equate Republican electoral success with burgeoning public support for values of moralism, traditionalism, and religion is a mistake.

Our values data indicate that between 1992 and 2004, Americans on the whole registered declining interest in institutions: family, church, and state. This change is manifested in declining scores on several key values at the top of the map. As we saw in the Introduction, values here are associated with deference to authority, which tends to entail adherence to traditional social roles and attachment to traditional institutions. Those whose values place them at the top of the map are generally devoted to order in many forms: they appreciate stability, predictability, and ritual. Here we find an attachment to national order, including the belief that immigrants should assimilate to the culture of their adoptive country and leave their old ways behind (we call this value *Cultural Assimilation*). We also find an ardent belief in familial order: a family is a married man and woman with children, and Dad is the boss and principal breadwinner *(Traditional Family)*. Familial order in turn hinges on sexual order: people should adhere to traditional gender roles and avoid any experimentation in dress, behaviour, or relationships *(Traditional Gender Identity)*. Finally, there is a devotion to a generalized sense of social order: people should practise courtesy and respect the rules of propriety *(Propriety)*.

At the top of the map, then, good fences make good neighbours, clothes make the man, and a rod unspared means a child unspoiled. One of George W. Bush's first acts as president was to impose a suit-and-tie dress code at the White House. This highly symbolic rule showed his conservative supporters that the new administration understood the rules of propriety. The Clinton years of wonks in khakis and late-night presidential pizza parties were over, and with them the moral slippage that follows the relaxing of rules, even rules that seem trivial. The military also comes to mind, where chores like scrubbing a floor with a toothbrush or making a latrine sparkle, seemingly irrelevant to the job of winning a war or defending a territory, in fact make a large group of individuals develop a sense of rigid order and collective effort. Thus, such tasks, when undertaken with sufficient gravity and intensity, actually underpin the *social* order that more directly serves the institution's goals.

Our values data over the '92 to '04 period indicate that belief in the kind of propriety projected by the Bush White House has been declining among ordinary Americans, along with the dutiful, orderly values that lie behind all those blue suits and red ties. But if these values are in decline, why would a president who espouses them so ostentatiously be elected? A fair question I will soon attempt to answer.

Another prominent example that would seem to contradict the evolution I describe in Americans' values is the seeming groundswell of opposition to same-sex marriage. In all eleven states where voters were asked whether the constitution should be amended to prohibit such marriages, a majority voted for the amendment (and against same-sex marriage rights). Among these eleven states were two, Oregon and Michigan, that chose Kerry over Bush.

But the proportion of Americans we surveyed who agreed with the statement "Society should regard two people of the same sex who live together as being the same as a married couple" rose from 28 percent in 1992 to 45 percent in 2004—still not a majority, but a substantial trend toward acceptance. (Incidentally, this flexibility also applies to common-

AUTHORITY

Traditional Family
Obedience to Authority   Religiosity
Propriety
National Pride
Duty

SURVIVAL

FULFILLMENT

INDIVIDUALITY

Authority Trends, 2004 Positions

law partners; agreement with the statement "Society should regard people who live together without being married as a family" rose from 49 to 57 percent from '92 to '04. Yes, these are the American numbers, not those we gathered in liberal Canada or the decadent Netherlands.)

Opponents of same-sex marriage are vocal and politically mobilized, and they do enjoy considerable popular support, but the image of Americans outside New York and California rising up with one angry voice against gay unions is an illusion. Indeed, the language that people use to describe the issues exercises huge influence on Americans' views. While the word *marriage* is fiercely contested territory, close to half of even self-identified *Republicans* support civil unions for same-sex couples. And Americans' growing acceptance of same-sex unions, despite much bluster from opponents, is unlikely to abate. Among Americans under thirty, a majority support same-sex marriage—and that's *marriage* marriage, not separate-but-equal marital unions.

There's no doubt that religion, patriotism, and perhaps most topically the traditional definition of marriage remain important forces in American culture and politics. It's little wonder that some in middle America long for those good old days evoked in the movies we pull out on Christmas Eve. After all, they live in a country that offers pay-per-view porn in every hotel room and whose sin city Las Vegas rivals Bangkok for its lascivious attractions—sex, gambling, drugs, you name it. But the idea that Americans in general are flocking to traditional values anew after a series of lonely and godless "me" decades is false. In fact, values related to traditional authority have been declining or holding steady over the past twelve years and the hedonism of the me decades is very much alive in "conservative" America.

THOSE OTHER MORAL VALUES

In the wake of the 2004 election, cognitive linguist George Lakoff published an article in *The Nation* entitled "Our Moral Values." Lakoff's interest is primarily in the linguistic "framing" of political issues—how the words politicians use to describe an issue are just the tip of an immense iceberg of meaning in listeners' minds. The point of Lakoff's article was that Americans' association of "moral values" with Republican issues—the opposition to abortion and gay marriage, the promotion of abstinence from sex in schools, and so on—is an instance of framing. Democrats fight for other causes—economic equality, racial justice, the protection of the environment—precisely because they believe these goals are morally important. But these Democratic issues aren't framed as moral issues, and Lakoff seeks to explain why and to help Democrats reframe the debate.

It's helpful to focus on the idea that meaning and morality do not reside exclusively at the top of the map—among the moral values of *Duty, Traditional Family, National Pride,* and *Religiosity.* Certainly, the top of the map offers a coherent system of meaning to which many Americans, and many people around the world, are deeply attached. There is, however, another site of meaning represented on the social values map: the right-hand (Fulfillment) pole.

This side of the map is intent on the quest for personal fulfillment as felt and understood by the individual. But the right quadrants offer two versions of this world view: fulfillment sought in concert with the authority-related values at the top of the map, or independent of them at the bottom.

For example, in the upper-right quadrant we find the trend *Everyday Ethics*. This value, which measures people's commitment to ethical conduct even in minor daily matters, has both a deferential component and a personal one. It signals an adherence to an absolute moral code (affirmed by religion, political authority, and social norms), but it also contains an element of personal integrity: people strong on this value do the right thing even when wrongdoing couldn't possibly be discovered, because their personal fulfillment relies in part on their own right conduct. Oscar Wilde said, "The nicest feeling in the world is to do a good deed anonymously, and have someone find out." For the Americans in the upper-right quadrant, the good deed is its own reward—really. (Soccer moms and dads who coach Little League know this intuitively.)

At the *bottom* right of the map, by contrast, we find the trend *Flexible Families*. This value measures respondents' acceptance of non-traditional family models, including same-sex and common-law unions. *Flexible Families* is at odds with the dictates of authority: traditional authority, religious authority, and if those favouring the constitutional amendment get their way, political authority. So it's predictable that this trend should be located at the bottom of the map, far away from trends associated with deference to authority. And *Flexible Families* is found at the right of the map because it's associated with a personal quest for fulfillment as defined by one's own standards, not those of other people. People who score high on the value *Flexible Families* believe that individuals should be free to construct the families they find sustaining, regardless of the imperatives of traditional social norms. These people believe that a gay couple, if they wished and were allowed by the state, would raise as happy and productive (and straight) a child as a straight couple.

It's also, by the way, in this lower-right area of the map that the average Canadian and Western European is found. Gertrude Himmelfarb writes in her book *One Nation, Two Cultures* that "If some of the effects of [the cultural revolution of the 1960s]—single-parenthood or out-of-wedlock births, for example—do not occupy Europeans as much as they do Americans (with the exception of the English, who are much troubled by them), this may reflect the ethos of those countries more than objective

conditions." True enough. Societies that evolve into the lower-right quadrant have totally different standards from societies at the top of the map.
They may "suffer" from what top-of-map types would deem social "ills"
like overt homosexuality, high divorce rates, flagrant teenage sexuality, and
so on. But the world view of the lower-right quadrant doesn't tend to see
these as ills because it operates in a different framework from the one
found at the top of the map. Moreover, America is *not* evolving into the
lower-right quadrant in the manner of Europeans and Canadians; it's
moving down the map into the lower-left quadrant, which produces
some—but certainly not all—of the same social results.

Although the values at the right of the map are organized around
personal fulfillment, the principle at work here is not mere selfishness. In
this area of the map, the individual quest for *meaning* is prized, not just
the individual quest for pleasure or gain. And whether personal meaning
is derived from traditional, authority-oriented sources at the top of the
map or more flexible, idiosyncratic sources at the bottom, "meaning" is a
deep and genuine quest. It may not unfold along a traditional religious
course, but it does seek to construct an authentic framework that encom-
passes pleasure, morality, community, and spirituality.

The right side of the map—even the bottom right—is not home to the
"if it feels good, do it" crowd that so distresses moralists. Instead we find
people who are likely to agree with such statements as "It's very important
to me to be able to communicate with people sincerely and sponta-
neously" (one of the items from *Personal Expression*); "I would like to
arrange my work schedule so that, if important personal matters need
attention, I'm free to attend to them and work at a later time" *(Meaningful
Moments);* "I like to put myself in another person's shoes and imagine how
I would have felt in his or her place" *(Introspection and Empathy);* and "I
often contemplate the meaning of my life" *(Spiritual Quest).* These trends
are introspective but not selfish; they reflect a flexible, personally defined
quest for meaning but not a set of priorities that is amoral or ignores
others' needs. Not necessarily religious, those on the right of the map may
well ask what Jesus would do in a given situation—but would be unlikely
to cite a particular scriptural passage or papal edict in explaining their

action, preferring to aim for the spirit rather than the letter of the law. (After asking what Jesus would do, they might also muse about the Buddha's position, and ask a friend whether Talmud had anything to say on the matter.)

Having gained a sense of the values found at the Fulfillment end of the map, let's look at how right-of-map values have fared during the 1992–2004 period.

In two words, not well. These "other moral values" are faring no better than the traditional ones at the top of the map. The trend *Introspection and Empathy*, which measures respondents' interest in understanding themselves better and empathizing with others, declined significantly from 1992 to 2004. This trend is crucial to the right-of-map world view, given that self-awareness is the foundation of an individual's quest for meaning.

Similarly, *Spiritual Quest* has declined significantly. Located in the upper-right quadrant but lower down and farther right than *Religiosity* (that is, in a more individualistic and fulfillment-oriented space on the map), the value *Spiritual Quest* registers people's commitment to seeking meaning in life through spiritual exploration, whether through a religious community and organized religious practice or through exposure to diverse theological ideas and faith practices. In 1992 the proportion of Americans saying that it was becoming more important to them "to have a more intense and more spiritual inner life" was 53. By 2004 that proportion had dropped fifteen points to 38 percent. If empathic Oprah was the 1990s, the more judgmental Dr. Phil (her spin-off protégé) is the 2000s.

Traditionalists and cynics might see declining scores on *Spiritual Quest* merely as a symptom of Americans' becoming less flaky. Those who take more cues from the Madonna than from Madonna (the one from Michigan) might be forgiven for wondering whether it's really very worrisome that the average American is less intent on pursuing a flavour-of-the-month spiritual fad ("Yoga is so '90s; I'm deeply into kabbalah; numerology is so … *real*, you know?"). But the value *Spiritual Quest* is not an index of how many Americans are two-weekend-a-year Buddhists; it's an index of whether Americans are seeking deep meaning in their lives.

A byproduct of such a quest is the espousal of values rooted in considered beliefs, not just in the pursuit of jolts and thrills or victory in winner-take-all contests. Combined with declining scores on *Introspection and Empathy*, diminishing *Spiritual Quest* signals a decline in one important practice individuals can undertake as a step toward engaging with others in a thoughtful, positive way.

The right-of-map value *Personal Expression* is likewise in decline. *Personal Expression* measures respondents' desire to be able to communicate deeply and authentically with others. The item from this trend that has declined most sharply asks respondents whether it's important to them "to develop my personality and be able to express it better." The falling rate of agreement with this item is consistent with the declining interest in intro-spection, spiritual exploration, and deep meaning we find in other values.

It's interesting that even a trend like *Sensualism* has declined. That the proportion of Americans saying "I love situations in which I can completely relax, such as taking a hot bath" has gone down from 1992 to 2004 may seem a trivial finding. But diminishing interest in what some might call "mindfulness"—taking time to relax and pay attention to an experience, even something as simple as a bath—is a notable development when viewed in combination with the other changes we see in the American values profile. Not to mention the fact that Americans, unlike Europeans, are working over 200 hours (five weeks) more per year than in 1973, and have less and less time for all kinds of personal activities from which people derive satisfaction: spending time with family, reading, volunteering, exercising, meditating, or praying. Europeans pretend to work a thirty-five-hour week, the joke goes, while Americans strive for the thirty-five-hour day. (And with ever better mobile communications facilitating Herculean multitasking, they may yet make it.) In a time-stressed world, few have time for a tub, and the vast majority opt instead for a quick shower before rushing off to work or to shop. But bathtubs don't seem to disappear from home design. Like similarly disused living rooms, they remain to fill a symbolic or aspirational role—patiently awaiting the day when their exhausted owners will slip into them and start living the lives they work so hard to achieve.

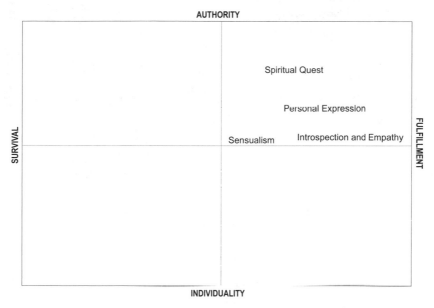

Introspective Trend, 2004 Position

Overall, then, the Fulfillment end of the map is losing its grip in much the same way as the Authority end. The average American is rejecting personal definitions of and quests for meaning. This rejection of right-of-map fulfillment values is one of three factors driving Americans' movement on the values map. The second factor is the decline in authority-oriented values at the top of the map. The third, and most important, is the significant growth in numerous values in the *Exclusion and Intensity* quadrant, especially values associated with sensation and thrill-seeking and with Darwinism and exclusion. Americans' increased attraction to the values of the lower-left quadrant, combined with their increasing indifference to values at the top and right of the map (which might loosely be called conservative and liberal, respectively), produces the trajectory we see in this map.

But embedded in this somewhat bleak picture of the 1992–2004 trajectory is another story—a shift that occurred between 2000 and 2004. Only time will allow us to fully understand and contextualize this shift as either a jog in Americans' continued descent into the lower-left quadrant or the beginning of another plot twist in the story of America.

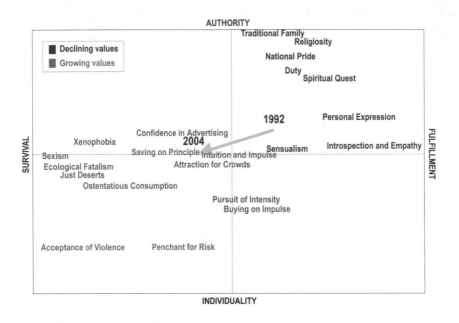

THE POST-9/11 PERIOD

I set out to write a book about America several years ago. My colleagues and I had amassed three waves of social values surveys and we thought we had some interesting findings. After a year of crunching data and applying our 1992, 1996, and 2000 research to our work with clients, we scheduled a meeting to discuss how our story of social change might fit into a book. The meeting was scheduled for 1:00 P.M. on September 11, 2001.

Of course the sheer human horror of the day overwhelmed any discussion we might have had. Like so many millions of Americans, our entire office sat glued to the TV in the boardroom until we could endure the terrible news loop no longer and each drifted home from work, much as we had from school on November 22, 1963, on the day President Kennedy was assassinated in Dallas. But as well as the emotional shock there was the knowledge that while our most recent survey in 2000 didn't seem very old on September 10, it seemed hopelessly dated, even void, on September 11. The book project was shelved, and America and the rest of the world moved forward into what came to be known as "the new normal."

Our 2004 survey, fielded in the summer, afforded us the opportunity to look in on Americans' values at what I think was a fortuitous moment. For one thing, it was three years after the terrible day that some said would change everything forever, at a time when the immediate visceral jolt had subsided but the new normal (with its greater attention to personal and national security and its war on terror) was firmly in place. What's more, Americans were ramping up to the 2004 presidential election. Thus, they were reflecting on the changes of the foregoing four years, and considering whether they thought this *particular* new normal, directed by the Bush administration, was the right one for America.

Values are deep-seated and do not fluctuate according to the events of the day. But certainly the mood of the nation can change drastically overnight. In fact, the mood of the entire world can change in an hour or two. In the wake of 9/11, the prestigious *Le Monde* of Paris declared, "Nous sommes tous Américains." One hundred thousand Canadians gathered on their nation's Parliament Hill and, openly weeping, deposited a mountain of flowers on the nearby steps of the U.S. embassy in Ottawa. To say 9/11 changed the mood of the world is to understate the sudden shock, sadness, anger, and fear that descended on that day. But for the purposes of differentiating the feelings of the moment from abiding values, I will refer to this change as a change in *mood*.

Opinions can also change rapidly. The George Bush Jr. who had heretofore seemed a little aimless was suddenly, if belatedly, confirmed as president. After 9/11, "W," whether walking through the rubble of Ground Zero or addressing the nation in pained but certain tones, became the President—a platform from which he would soon ascend (literally, in a flight suit) to the identity of Commander-in-Chief. The mortal man became the iconic office, seemingly overnight. In crisis, individuals become more deferential. After 9/11, public approval of Bush, which until then had hovered around half, soared to 90 percent and remained over 70 percent for nearly a year. Surely many people who hadn't voted for Bush, and had maybe even questioned the legitimacy of his victory, found that their opinions of the man changed when he became the Man (at least symbolically) standing between them and a world that seemed suddenly dangerous and full of malicious enemies (yet again).

Values are not as mutable as moods or opinions, but they are certainly shaped by events in the world. One's upbringing, education, and relationships affect one's values, as do broader economic circumstances, wars, and cultural moments. Think of those who grew up in the Great Depression saving string and rubber bands in their well-appointed homes five decades later; their values were shaped by an experience of profound and lasting deprivation, and no matter how circumstances may improve, those values remain. Or boomers who came of age in the 1960s: they may have gotten jobs and haircuts, and they may have emulated their parents by getting married, having kids, and even moving to the suburbs, but their attitudes about authority, religion, community, fairness, consumption, family, and gender bear the traces of their experiences. People's values evolve gradually over time, but they don't manifest the wide swings that moods and opinions do.

People can also change the *emphasis* they place on values. When crisis strikes, people pull together. Family, already important, becomes even more cherished. Every weekend is Thanksgiving weekend, at least for a while. We look to our leaders and those entrusted with our protection for leadership and bravery. The NYPD, the firefighters, Dad, the president. Traditional manly virtues are revalued. After a decade of fooling around (and not just in the Oval Office) it is now time to get back to basics. The institutions neglected amid the forces of individualism and hedonism suddenly regain their importance. The values that had made America a great nation—the American Dream, the resolute belief that any problem can be solved, that any enemy can be vanquished—re-emerge. Religion offers solace, ritual, and meaning.

Some have likened 9/11, in its emotional impact on Americans collectively, to a death in the family—the death, more specifically, of a young person: unexpected, unnatural, particularly traumatic. I think this metaphor is apt, and it sheds light on what the terrorist attacks could and could not do to America. When there's a death in the family, emotions certainly change; people are sobered and feel vulnerable, they come together. Plans change: the trip to Vegas suddenly seems trivial, even crass; a trip to church seems more appropriate. Perhaps family tensions are, for a time, quieted. You may not get along with your brother or your dad, but he's going through the same terrible experience you are—and after all, you're still family. The family's deeper values are unlikely to change; there's too much shared history for that. And usually, with time, people will get over the loss—they won't forget it, but their lives will resume their usual rhythms. Maybe the trip to Vegas will reappear on the family calendar in a few years; old tensions will re-emerge; the sense of solidarity will dissipate.

It is too soon to say if 9/11 has had an impact on the values of Americans on a scale or depth equivalent to the Great Depression of the 1930s or the affluent society of 1950s, but that day certainly helped inspire the political expression of many Americans' new emphasis on traditional values and institutions. George W. Bush became to post-9/11 America what FDR became on that other date in infamy, the surprise bombing of Pearl Harbor on December 7, 1941. Bush was transformed from a so-so president into the politically invincible leader of a country at war. Come 2004, the Democrats nominated John Kerry, a man many thought was a genuine war hero, who ostentatiously "reported for duty" in speeches. But this seaman was fighting not just an incumbent at a time of war but a visceral retrenchment to traditional authority among the voting public.

So the values in the United States between 2000 and 2004 did register a shift, evident in the average American's position on the social values map.

That the average American moved left and *up* from 2000 to 2004 is the result of three shifts in values: (1) a freeze on the growth of many of the *Exclusion and Intensity* values I described in the early part of this chapter; (2) a resurgence in some quintessentially American values,

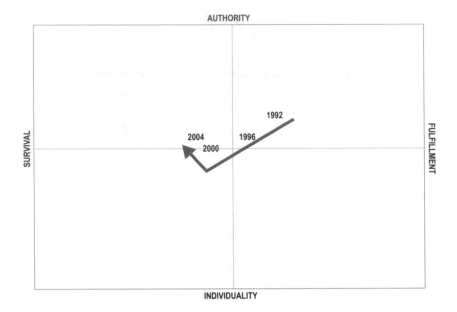

including aspiration, industry, and optimism; and (3) a renewed interest in connecting with other people, both locally and, remarkably, globally.

The table below shows that growth in many of the *Exclusion and Intensity* trends not only stalled in the post-9/11 period but in a few cases even *reversed*. Similarly, declines in some of the authority and (less so) fulfillment values, at the top and the right of the map respectively, also froze in the 2000–2004 period.

	1992–2004	2000–2004
THRILLS AND INTENSITY		
Intuition and Impulse	142	100
Attraction for Crowds	160	109
Pursuit of Intensity	124	95
Penchant for Risk	193	113
DARWINISM AND EXCLUSION		
Xenophobia	163	118
Sexism	156	93

Ecological Fatalism	169	123
Acceptance of Violence	256	92
CONSUMPTION		
Confidence in Advertising	136	107
Saving on Principle	192	100
Ostentatious Consumption	138	92
Buying on Impulse	118	93
AUTHORITY AND TRADITION		
Traditional Family	85	106
Religiosity	71	96
Duty	64	108
National Pride	42	66
FULFILLMENT AND AUTONOMY		
Spiritual Quest	43	46
Personal Expression	46	67
Introspection and Empathy	56	90
Sensualism	61	94

Change scores; 100 signifies no change; higher signifies growth, lower signifies decline[7]

Above we see at the very least a shift in emphasis, if not a deeper shift in the values evolution of Americans. The huge reversal in *Acceptance of Violence* is particularly telling: violence may have seemed fun and exciting when stylized in video games and Hollywood explosions, but in the minds of many Americans a real attack on its civilians and a real war have turned violence from titillating to horrifying. This shift is emblematic of an overall sobering of Americans' values in the post 9/11 period.

Just as they got more serious about the meaning of violence, Americans also got more serious about work. Between 2000 and 2004, Americans' scores on such values as *Work Ethic, Entrepreneurialism,* and *Personal Challenge* increased. Consistent with these developments, the trend *American Dream* also grew. In 2000, over eight in ten Americans (81 percent) already agreed with the statement "I believe in the American Dream: it's possible for anyone in this country to have success if they reach for it." The proportion agreeing somewhat or strongly rose to 85 percent in 2004, but the proportion agreeing strongly rose from 38 to 48 percent. In other words, nearly half of all Americans in 2004 believed *strongly* that Abe Lincoln's climb from the log cabin to the White House or Oprah's ascent from rags to riches was still possible in their country—still possible for them, their children, or the child of the poorest family in the nation.

Americans' faith in the private sector has also risen. Asked whether business should have more or less power in society, Americans were more likely in 2004 than in 2000 to say it should have *more*—and this even despite the high-profile corporate governance scandals (Enron, WorldCom, Tyco, Martha) of the previous several years.

Meanwhile, even amid a war and a period of considerable government activism, Americans say that politics and politicians should exert *less* influence in society. This finding may be related to those of the Pew Center, according to which 64 percent of Americans in May 2005 believed that members of the two political parties were "bickering more than usual"; only 41 percent said the same thing in May 2001. And those who thought politicians were "working together more than usual" in May 2005 numbered a mere 13 percent. (Eight percent volunteered the response that the scene in Washington was business as usual.)

The second important strain of values on which Americans increased their scores between 2000 and 2004 involved interpersonal connections. After the national trauma of 9/11 and the security anxieties thereafter, it's no surprise that Americans would express a renewed attraction to connecting with those close to them. They registered a stronger focus on their families and communities *(Social Intimacy)*, and reported that they were paying extra attention to rites of passage and shared celebrations: births, comings of age, marriages, anniversaries, birthdays, graduations *(Celebrating Passages)*.

And this desire to connect wasn't limited only to family and friends. The post-9/11 period saw Americans expressing greater *Global Consciousness* and an increased interest in *Culture Sampling*. A cynic might say that this

Optimism and Aspiration Values, 2004 Positions

renewed interest in the world only reaffirms Ambrose Bierce's barb that "War is God's way of teaching Americans geography." The cynic, however, would be mistaken: Americans were showing not just greater *awareness* of the world but greater *empathy* for people in other parts of the planet. In 2004 three-quarters of Americans (74 percent) said they often or sometimes "feel what other countries are going through when I watch them on television (on the international news, for example)," a 10 percent increase from the year 2000. Similarly, Americans registered a strong interest in international travel: 77 percent in 2004 agreed that "I have an interest in travelling to and learning about other countries and their way of life," up 7 percent from 2000. This predilection for travel might be merely fanciful for many Americans, since according to the U.S. State Department's Bureau of Consular Affairs only 21 percent hold a valid passport. But an increasing proportion are acting on their curiosity: the same office reported that the 7,399,667 new and renewed passports issued in 2003 beat the last record, set in 2000. But among those who don't follow through and actually travel, the idea that Americans are even *reporting* greater interest in exploring the world in 2004 than in 2000 is a noteworthy development.

Social Openness Values, 2004 Positions

It's true that *Xenophobia* also increased somewhat between 2000 and 2004, but this trend was evident prior to 9/11. No doubt the 2001 terrorist attacks spurred some xenophobic outbursts (some targeted at Arab Americans), but no special or lasting upsurge of xenophobic sentiment is evident in our data when we compare the 2000 and 2004 surveys.

W E'VE SEEN that from 1992 to 2004 the gross movement of U.S. society has been into the *Exclusion and Intensity* quadrant—toward brutal competition, exclusion, thrills, and consumption and away from both the traditionalism at the top and the autonomous fulfillment-seeking at the right of the map. The 2000 to 2004 period, however, marked a shift in American values whose significance will be revealed only in the next several years. The apparent renewal of both American aspiration and Americans' openness to the world seems to speak to a deep sense of confidence and optimism—about America's prospects, about fairness in America, and about people in general around the globe. It represents a remarkable response to 9/11 and a testament to the resilience of the

American creed and its Dream. If it proves durable, it will certainly put the lie to those who claim that in a frenzy of fear (and in some cases loathing) Americans have drifted permanently away from the ideals and values that made their country great.

two

The Real Culture War: Either versus Neither

My fellow Americans, this is the most important election of our lifetime.
—Senator John Kerry at the Democratic National Convention, July 29, 2004

The election of 2004 is one of the most important,
not just in our lives, but in our history.
—Vice-President Dick Cheney at the Republican
National Convention, September 1, 2004

Voting is for old people.
—Urban Outfitters T-shirt, spring 2004

IT DIDN'T TAKE LONG for the T-shirt whose slogan is quoted above to be yanked from the shelves at Urban Outfitters. Concerned old people from across the political spectrum made loud objections to the garment, which they accused of encouraging apathy among non-old people. The shirt was called anti-American, anti-democratic, and an abomination.

Talk about ignorant armies clashing by night. Old, grave, fear-driven political culture meets young, ironic, fun-driven popular culture. Confusion reigns, laughter ceases, half feel mocked and the other half feel scolded. No wonder voting is for old people.

Jonah Goldberg of the *National Review* rightly points out that this saucy T-shirt was not alone on the shelves. It probably resided near the one that reads "Porn Star" or another that reads "Beer: It's What's for Breakfast." All the shirts are meant as jokes, he acknowledges, but why do Democrats stop laughing only when a shirt comes along that might compromise their youth votes? According to Goldberg, Democrats "don't care if kids get the message to be lazy, slutty drunks—so long as they vote." (Presumably lazy, slutty drunks vote Democrat.)

Of course, these shirts have as little to do with Democratic politics as they do with Republican politics. The real issue here is not whether Democrats spend less time than Republicans worrying about America's T-shirts, but why the mood of American politics is so at odds with the mood of so many American people, especially youth.

The reason for the disparate trajectories of social and political change is voter turnout. From the late 1970s to 2000 turnout in presidential elections tended to hover at just over half, the charged and crucial election of 2004 saw turnout surge to 60.3 percent of eligible voters. (It remains to be seen whether that 2004 turnout will prove a blip or something more.) And it goes without saying that in a country where only a little over half of eligible voters show up to the polls, it matters very much who shows up.[1]

When remarked upon at all by politicians, low turnout is usually used as fodder in partisan shouting matches. Liberals claim that ordinary Americans want greater economic equality, better health care, and other Democratic goods but are so downtrodden and hopeless, and so convinced that no one in power cares about them, that they assume there's no point in voting. Conservatives point to low turnout as a sign of voter disgust at Washington politicking (read: bloated liberal government). In this analysis, so many ordinary Americans don't vote because they're applying to their relationship with government their mothers' advice about how to deal with irritating siblings: "Just ignore them—or you'll only encourage them."

In fact, the values of non-voters suggest that neither of these analyses is true. Politically disengaged Americans aren't secretly longing for a more compassionate welfare state or smaller government. They're focused on their own individualistic pursuits: trying to get ahead financially and pursuing pleasure through entertainment, thrill-seeking, and consumption (conspicuous when possible). Civic duty, like other kinds of duty, is a dull relic to these Americans. In 2000, 40 percent of those who said they were unlikely to vote said they identify with "people who avoid jury duty and don't vote because citizenship and participation in government don't mean much any more." (By contrast, among people who said they would certainly vote, half that proportion—20 percent—expressed the same lack of faith in the importance of citizenship.) For many unlikely voters, unless it's going to mean ringside seats at another trial of the century (O.J., the Menendez brothers, Michael Jackson), jury duty is to be avoided. Voting is even easier to avoid; no one much cares whether you show up. (Unless you live in a swing county in Ohio, in which case you're likely to have a partisan volunteer parked in your driveway with the engine running throughout the month of October—just in case.)

In the last chapter, we saw how the values of the American population changed over the last twelve years (1992–2004) and outlined five categories of change: (1) increasing Darwinism, (2) increasing thrill-seeking, (3) increasing attraction to consumption, (4) declining attachment to authority and institutions, and (5) declining focus on fulfillment and the inner life. In all five of these categories, the values of the most politically engaged Americans (defined here as those who report that they're certain to vote in the next election) differ markedly from the population at large. The values of those who said they were *unlikely* to vote, however, matched the broader pattern of social change.

The point here is not that Americans are becoming increasingly disengaged politically as they adopt the values of the lower-left quadrant. Voter turnout rates, at least, would suggest otherwise: with the exception of the 10 point rise in 2004, turnout rates have been fairly stable, if low, since the late 1970s. Regardless of the long-term significance of the uptick in 2004, it seems clear that voter turnout is not in serious decline.

The point is, rather, that the values of American voters strikingly diverge from the values of Americans who don't vote and that this divergence is

increasing. Indeed, as we will see, American voters are on a trajectory of growing deference to authority, traditionalism, and conservatism—values that may even be read as a reaction against the overall trajectory of social change explored in the last chapter. In other words, voters in America (and thus presumably the candidates they're electing) are not so much representative of the nature of social change in the United States as they are a counterweight or a response to that change.

When we plot Certain Voters on the values map, their divergence from the American population at large is clear.

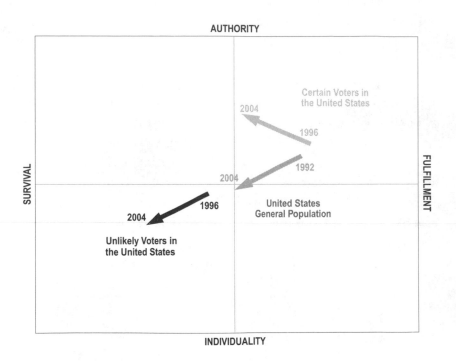

In the last chapter, we broke down the changes in values that are drawing the average American into the lower-left quadrant. It's useful here to look at those values again, and see how the scores of politically engaged and politically disengaged Americans differ on them.

The table on the next page displays index scores for three groups on the set of values described in the last chapter as driving American society's

movement down and left on the social values map. The three groups of Americans shown are the population at large, Americans who report that they're certain to vote, and those who report that they're unlikely to vote.

To some extent, the table compares apples and oranges. The scores for the general population register change over time; over 100 indicates that Americans on average were stronger on the trend in 2004 than in 1992 and under 100 indicates they were weaker. The scores for the Certain Voters and Unlikely Voters, however, are from 2004 only (that is, a score of over 100 indicates that the group in question was stronger on the trend than the general population was *in 2004 alone*).

It's impossible to show static 2004 numbers for the general population because index scores are comparative—we can't compare the population with itself (unless we compare it with itself at another time). But the comparison of the general population and the two voting groups in 2004 is embedded in the index scores of Certain and Unlikely voters in 2004. On *Acceptance of Violence*, for example, Certain Voters were weaker than the rest of Americans while Unlikely Voters were stronger. The column showing change scores for the general population offers additional information: it shows that in most cases the differences between Certain Voters and the general population are only growing. To take *Acceptance of Violence* as an example again, the change from 1992 to 2004 shows us that the population at large is growing stronger on this trend—which means that they're diverging from Certain Voters and converging with Unlikely Voters.

	U.S. Change 1992–2004	Certain to Vote 2004	Unlikely to Vote 2004
DARWINISM			
Acceptance of Violence	256	48	168
Penchant for Risk	193	60	165
Xenophobia	163	93	100
Ecological Fatalism	169	77	107
(Ecological Concern)	72	169	63
Sexism	156	81	107

THRILLS AND SENSATIONS			
Attraction for Crowds	160	96	117
Sexual Permissiveness	156	70	145
Intuition and Impulse	142	86	124
Pursuit of Intensity	124	72	120
Mysterious Forces	114	109	113
Penchant for Risk	193	60	165

CONSUMPTION			
Saving on Principle	192	104	92
Joy of Consumption	89	67	131
Ostentatious Consumption	138	73	136
Confidence in Advertising	136	72	159
Buying on Impulse	118	68	159
Discriminating Consumerism	72	169	60

REJECTION OF INSTITUTIONS			
Primacy of the Family	83	122	82
Duty	64	152	63
Religiosity	71	236	78
National Pride	42	164	61

INDIFFERENCE TO INNER LIFE			
Sensualism	61	89	113
Introspection and Empathy	56	143	78
Personal Expression	46	130	92
Spiritual Quest	43	140	100
Effort Toward Health	59	154	58

low (under 80)

neutral (80–120)

high (over 120)

While the average American moved away from traditionalism and moralism between 1992 and 2004, the American *voter* moved up the map toward exactly those values, becoming more strongly attached to patriotism, religion, the traditional family, and personal duty. This trajectory is instructive when considered alongside the percentage increase in George W. Bush's popular vote from the 2000 election to that of 2004. After the 2004 election most explanations of the Bush victory focused on one of three things: security, moral values, and campaign technique (including messaging, organization, and mobilization).

"Before you come up, dear, don't forget to secure the perimeter."

Exit polls found that voters most concerned about security voted Bush. Similarly, those who saw the war in Iraq as a front in the war on terror voted Bush, and those who doubted that Iraq had much to do with 9/11 or averting future terror attacks tended to vote Kerry.

To many, 2004 seemed to be the year of moral values. Karl Rove reputedly drew millions of religious conservatives out of the woodwork to vote for Bush by stressing threats to their Bible-believing ideals, especially same-sex marriage and abortion. And although *The Economist* pointed out after the election that the 22 percent of voters citing "moral values" as their top concern in the election was actually *lower* than the analogous proportions in 2000 (35 percent) and 1996 (40 percent), there is no doubt that in the tooth-and-nail 2004 election, getting a few million moralist voters to the polls was an enormous contribution to the Bush victory.

But some Democrats have argued that rather than its actual policies, it was the effectiveness and discipline of Republican messaging that proved crucial in the last election. George Lakoff has observed that linguistic "framing" of issues by Republicans, and Democrats' unwitting acceptance of those powerful frames, puts Democrats on Republican turf before the debate has even begun. "Let me tell you why I oppose *tax relief* and favour *partial-birth abortion*": political suicide.

Each of these factors was surely important in the last presidential election, and none shows any sign of disappearing from the American political discussion any time soon. But few on either side of the political spectrum have ventured the hypothesis that American voters as a whole are actually becoming decidedly more conservative. Not just circling the wagons after 9/11, not just being swayed by an increasingly confident and vocal hard right, not just responding to a well-oiled conservative movement (and a stalled liberal one), but at the level of personal values becoming profoundly more attached to tradition, institutions, and authority. According to our values surveys, American voters' movement up and left on the map, toward more traditional social values, is a crucial factor in the ascendancy of conservative politics in the United States. And the movement began long before 9/11. Our own data trace this current back to 1996, when we began our political tracking, and electoral politics suggests that the arrow on our map may have set out on its present course prior to the election of Ronald Reagan in 1980.

ABOUT THAT CULTURE WAR ...

I argued in the last chapter that Republican moralists who cast stones at the indulgent, amoral values that American popular culture seems so often to peddle misunderstand the forces they're fighting, and that it's not engaged Democrats who are leading the charge, as conservative writer Robert Bork would say, to Gomorrah. Indeed, a look at the values of politically engaged Republicans and Democrats reveals huge swaths of sameness. Although the more outrageous rhetoric of the 50–50 nation would suggest that Democrats and Republicans have nothing in common, those who even care to identify themselves as one or the other, and mark an X—any X—on election day, have vastly more in common with each other than they do with non-voters.

Think of the images of election day in 2004. Queues of voters snaking around blocks; elderly people in southern states being shaded from the sun by younger relatives or volunteers; high school gyms, libraries, and community centres swamped with huge diversities of people, each seeking to cast a single ballot. In some locations, voters spent most of their day lined up. Naturally, many of these people would have disagreed about the issues had they begun to discuss them with their queue mates. But some deep belief in the system, in the importance of voting, and in the power of political processes to effect meaningful change kept them all there, in line, for hours. I imagine one voter waiting to cast her vote in support of the troops in Iraq (that is, in support of the war on terror and the decisions of her incumbent commander-in-chief), and the next waiting for his chance to support the troops by voting against an administration that sent them to Iraq to root out nonexistent WMDs. But as different as these two people may be, in their values they *both* differ much more from those who shrug that a foreign war has nothing to do with them and why should they waste a day waiting to vote about it. Or, for that matter, about the environment, the economy, same-sex marriage, abortion, taxes, education, health care, Supreme Court nominations, America's place in the world, homeland security, civil rights, gun control ... the indifference goes on.

If we examine the values of Americans who say they're certain to vote, we find that they differ in three main areas from those who are unlikely to vote. First is their ideas about how they connect with others: their interpersonal relationships and their modes of community engagement. Second is their approach to matters of individualism and personal identity, including work, health, and spirituality. And third is the values they hold relating to social organization: family, religion, authority, multiculturalism, and propriety.

But when we go on to look at the values of Democrats and Republicans in these areas, we find that although the camps differ in their approaches to some of the matters just listed, they share a commitment to some version of each of the three concepts: community, individualism, and social organization. The politically disengaged, on the other hand, demonstrate little interest in *any* of these ideals. For them it isn't a war between communitarian and authoritarian values or between moralism and individualism; it is, at bottom, a war of all against all.

CONNECTION AND COMMUNITY

Community, like culture, has become a ubiquitous buzzword. Everything these days seems to constitute one: there are not only geographic communities but ethnic communities, religious communities, professional communities, online communities, hobby-based communities, and sports communities. It sometimes seems that the more people talk about communities the less they actually belong to them. After all, the more time we spend with our highly specialized segments of society—keeping in touch with the Dungeons and Dragons community online or staying abreast of the extreme mountain biking community on some obscure satellite channel—the less time we spend on the front porch chatting with neighbours (if one's home is even so old-fashioned as to have a front porch—or neighbours, for that matter).

The group of values I call "community-related" revolve around how people interact with each other (and their environment) in non-work settings. These values pertain to close personal relationships as well as to civic involvement, ethics, and attitudes toward the natural environment. On a number of these values Americans who say they're certain to vote score considerably higher than those who say they're unlikely to vote. In other words, politically engaged Americans aren't just more interested in political issues but appear to feel more strongly connected to other people, both those close to them and those in society at large.

Certain Voters are much stronger than average on *Civic Engagement,* indicating that they're interested in politics and feel a sense of duty toward such civic activities as voting and jury duty. Republicans somewhat exceed Democrats on *Civic Engagement,* but both groups are above average. There has been much self-flagellation among Democrats in recent elections (although not after the monumental effort of 2004) about Republicans' superior organization and discipline in getting out the vote. But to be fair, since Republicans tend to be stronger on top-of-map values like *Duty,* Republican organizers have a natural edge. Even if Republican voters don't particularly like their candidate or feel strongly about the issues at stake in a given race, they're simply more likely than Democrats to feel obligated to schlep to the polls on voting day.

Certain Voters on both sides of the partisan divide also have high scores on the trend *Meaningful Moments.* These Americans try to take time to cultivate meaningful connections with other people, even strangers they happen to meet in a day. Moreover, they report that they try to organize their lives so that if an important personal matter comes up, they can attend to it right away.

The fact that both Republicans and Democrats[2] score well above average on these two trends suggests that politically engaged Americans, whatever their ideology, not only feel connected to their society by civic duty but make an effort to foster a kind of emotional goodwill toward those around them. This brand of engagement, constituted of personal responsibility to others and a general interpersonal openness, might be considered the bedrock of strong communities.

From here, nuances of difference begin to emerge in the values Democrats and Republicans espouse vis-à-vis community. Democrats tend to be stronger on *Culture Sampling, Community Involvement,* and *Ecological Concern. Culture Sampling* measures openness to and curiosity about cultures other than one's own; Democrats are more likely than Republicans to agree, for example, that "I like to experience the customs and cultures of other peoples." But the politically disengaged are less likely than either Democrats or Republicans to take an interest in learning about other cultures. A high score on *Community Involvement* indicates that Democrats are especially likely to report that they volunteer, attend political meetings, and discuss neighbourhood issues with others. Democrats' higher score on *Ecological Concern* registers a belief that the environment shouldn't be automatically sacrificed for the sake of jobs and economic concerns, and that the environmental movement is a reasonable—not an extremist—project.

The values on which Republicans most markedly outstrip Democrats are *Social Intimacy* and *Everyday Ethics*. The higher *Social Intimacy* score indicates a stronger desire for close-knit, intimate communities, while a higher score on *Everyday Ethics* shows a greater commitment to rule-following and right conduct. As noted earlier, this trend speaks both to the deferential attitudes found at the top of the map (in this case deference to rules about honesty and fair dealing) and to the fulfillment-oriented mindset at the right of the map (those strongest on *Everyday Ethics* practise honesty even when rule-breaking is unlikely to be discovered, because honesty accords with their self-image and their self-respect).

Here again, though, the difference between Republicans and Democrats is less than that between the politically engaged and the disengaged. For example, respondents were asked the following question: "When the bill arrives, you discover that the waiter has forgotten to include your bar order. Do you tell the waiter about the mistake or do you quietly pay and leave?" Engaged Republicans emerge as the most honest on this item, with fewer than one in five (18 percent) saying they would just pay the (incomplete) bill and slip away. Engaged Democrats are only slightly less squeaky clean, with 23 percent reporting that they'd pay and leave. Among those who report that they're unlikely to vote, however, the proportion who would keep quiet about the miscalculation is over one-third (36 percent)—double the Republican proportion.

Certainly, these data reveal interesting differences between the values, and in particular the communitarian ideals, of Republicans and Democrats. Both groups are attached to these ideals, even though the particulars of the communities differ. Demographic studies of partisanship in the United States find that Republicans are more rural while Democrats are more urban. (In the 2000 election, counties that voted Democrat were on average three times as populous as Republican counties; Democratic "landslide" counties, where the Democrats won by more than 20 percentage points, were *eight* times more populous than Republican landslide counties.)[3] This accords with the visions of community life that emerge in the values of the two groups: Democrats, strong on *Culture Sampling,* tend to envision communities as sites of diversity and exchange where *Community Involvement* (neighbourhood meetings, volunteering) brings different groups together to shape a vibrant and workable community. Republicans tend more strongly to envision communities as places of intimacy and trust *(Social Intimacy)* where a sense of belonging and goodwill derives from shared codes of acceptable conduct *(Everyday Ethics).*

But Republicans and Democrats both emphasize the importance of community and approach social life in a spirit of responsibility and goodwill. Unlikely voters, meanwhile, generally demonstrate relatively little attachment to the community-oriented values of either partisan group.

Trend	Certain Voters	Democrats (Certain Voters)	Republicans (Certain Voters)	Unlikely Voters
Civic Engagement	277	148	177	38
Everyday Ethics	246	123	159	38
Meaningful Moments	194	141	130	63
Ecological Concern	169	173	74	60
Culture Sampling	137	143	91	68
Community Involvement	120	133	82	82
Social Intimacy	119	100	135	74

■ low (under 80)

■ neutral (80–120)

□ high (over 120)

PERSONAL IDENTITY

The trends under this heading address many aspects of identity, including autonomous behaviour, personal well-being, and religious belief. On several of these trends—the ones that centre on the ideal of personal control and agency—we find politically engaged Republicans and Democrats differing only minimally. Both groups report making a conscious effort to remain healthy and fit (the value *Effort Toward Health*). Both also say they feel more confident, happier, more likely to succeed, and better about themselves overall when they make sure they're looking their best *(Look Good Feel Good)*. Whether "their best" means a blue suit and tie, a crisp military uniform, or a more casual ensemble will depend on the occasion, of course, but also on their values. The common thread is an emphasis on putting their best foot forward; the threads themselves will differ.

Both groups register an interest in making thoughtful and informed choices in their consumer purchases *(Discriminating Consumerism)*. And when it comes to their personal affairs (managing their finances, researching health concerns and options online, and so on), engaged members of both parties say they try to do as much as they can on their own and, when they must hire professionals, try to collaborate with and learn from them *(Selective Use of Professional Services)*. Finally, both groups say they place a high premium on personal effort and initiative at work and school, and that they try to instill a strong work ethic in their children *(Work Ethic)*.

The combination of the discriminating consumerism and the do-it-yourself tendencies that we find among politically engaged Americans is likely a strong contributor to the shift in the consumer marketplace toward professional-quality gear for non-professionals. For Americans who are serious about cooking, it's not enough to have a stove—it has to be the same stove the best chefs on earth use. For those passionate about cycling, it's not enough to have a bike; it has to be a bike Lance Armstrong would be happy to ride. The same goes for tools, camping gear, computers, cameras, and anything else one might acquire as a hobbyist. (Actually, there's almost no such animal as a hobbyist in America these days; there are professionals with top-of-the-line gear who happen to have totally unrelated day jobs.)

Where Republicans and Democrats differ is on some values related to personal autonomy and identity. Republicans stand out on two strains here: those values associated with well-being and those associated with rules. Politically engaged Republicans place an emphasis on well-being in all areas of life: physical, material, and spiritual. They are especially strong on *Effort Toward Health*. And given their more conservative image, it's surprising perhaps that Republicans are also stronger than Democrats on the trend *Holistic Health,* suggesting they believe that health isn't merely a matter of the body but also of mind and spirit. Strong on *Financial Security,* Republicans feel confident in their financial well-being and see their *Work Ethic* as a source of their material comfort. *Religiosity* is the third pillar in the Republican triad of wellness; for many, religion is the moral and spiritual fount from which all other wellness flows. In his classic film *Annie Hall,* after being accused of stereotyping a fellow Jew, Woody Allen's character explains, "I'm a bigot, but for the left." A conservative Republican who adheres to this coherent set of wellness-oriented values might similarly say, "I'm holistic, but for the right."

The values of politically engaged Republicans suggest that they place considerable emphasis on the individual's ability to conform to rules for proper behaviour. Strong on *Propriety* and *Emotional Control,* these Americans tend to believe there's a right and wrong way to act; restraint and self-discipline are hallmarks of character and lead to appropriate and respectable behaviour. The trend *Personal Control* in this context evokes Republicans' individualistic desire to maintain control over their own affairs as well as their belief in the disciplined handling of one's body, soul, family, and finances. The trend *Work Ethic,* strong among Republicans, again points to the rules (of honest labour and self-sufficiency) by which Republicans see upright people living their lives. And *Religiosity* provides the moral framework in which all this personal discipline is enforced.

Among Democrats we find trends strongly associated with autonomy and personal choice. High index scores on *Discriminating Consumerism, Religion à la Carte,* and *Selective Use of Professional Services* suggest that politically engaged Democrats seek opportunities for customization in all quarters of life. They want to be able to hand-pick options that suit them personally and not simply accept a generic bill of goods. Engaged Democrats want to be able to choose which products (and which features of those products) are most useful and provide the best value, not be beholden to a given brand; they want to be able to engage in spiritual practice the way they see fit, selecting the ritual, study, and community they find most fruitful; they want to be able to handle their own affairs where they're competent to do so and in other areas hire professionals who will cooperate and collaborate with them. In short, the politically engaged Democrat's approach to personal identity and development centres on choice.

Differences between engaged Democrats and Republicans, then, are greater in the values associated with personal autonomy than in those related to community. Nevertheless, here again the real gulf is between the engaged and the disengaged, as the chart below makes apparent.

Trend	Certain Voters	Democrats (Certain Voters)	Republicans (Certain Voters)	Unlikely Voters
Religiosity	236	117	220	39
Personal Control	209	94	169	50
Look Good Feel Good	188	136	145	62
Holistic Health	171	114	141	59
Discriminating Consumerism	169	125	111	60
Propriety	169	111	181	65
Emotional Control	167	100	186	76
Religion à la Carte	173	150	100	71
Effort Toward Health	154	125	147	61
Selective Use of Professional Services	144	131	123	73
Financial Security	141	86	153	77
Personal Expression	130	100	136	92
Work Ethic	127	110	132	87

low (under 80)

neutral (80–120)

high (over 120)

SOCIAL ORGANIZATION

Perhaps not surprisingly, it's on values associated with social organization that Democrats and Republicans diverge most sharply. The values of engaged Republicans in this area revolve around authority, tradition, order, and patriotism. The values of engaged Democrats, meanwhile, revolve around fairness and empathy.

Engaged Republicans' values interlock in a fairly rational and coherent system. They see social order deriving from the authority of church, state, and family and the rules prescribed by those institutions. The role of the individual is to behave in ways that respect and reinforce this authority. Here then we find the values *Obedience to Authority, Patriarchy,* and *Religiosity.* In this world view, fathers and religious leaders provide moral guidance to the individual, who in turn does his *Duty* and practises sound *Everyday Ethics.* Following the rules, the individual plays the roles that duty prescribes in the family *(Traditional Family, Traditional Gender Identity)* and in society at large *(Propriety).* Patriotism, manifested in the value *National Pride,* is among the duties prescribed by political authority figures. And finally, *Cultural Assimilation* is necessary if immigrants are to participate fully in American society, venerating and reinforcing this web of American institutions.

Among politically engaged Democrats, the idea of men and women observing traditional gender roles is less important than the idea of men and women being treated equally; this attitude is evident in Democrats' higher score on *Gender Parity.* The value *Social Responsibility* points to a Democratic belief that individuals are responsible not so much to authority figures who have power over them but to each other as equals. In order for individuals to understand their responsibilities in society, they must be able to understand the needs of others and to cogently articulate their own needs; this is the root of the trend *Introspection and Empathy,* on which Democrats are particularly strong. And empathy in this world view extends not only to other members of society but to the earth itself *(Ecological Concern);* the needs of the ecosystem must be considered as society sets its priorities. Here again the idea of fairness is evident. While the Republican social order is based on hierarchy, with nature being subordinate to human projects and destined for exploitation, the more heterarchical Democratic vision of social order sees nature as a crucial component of a system in which various needs must be balanced rather than subordinated to one another in a vertical chain of command.

In these two models of how humans might interact with each other and their environment, we find more than echoes of the archetypal male and female of myth and legend: man overpowering and bringing order to the world (preferably with a wise and just hand) and woman participating in an organic whole where balance and mutual care, not power and discipline, are the fundamental goods.

But despite these interesting differences between Democratic and Republican values, once more it's the politically engaged and the disengaged who are truly speaking different languages.

Trend	Certain Voters	Democrats (Certain Voters)	Republicans (Certain Voters)	Unlikely Voters
Religiosity	236	117	220	39
Everyday Ethics	246	123	185	58
Social Responsibility	167	164	125	47
Traditional Family	200	100	254	47
Ecological Concern	169	173	74	60
Propriety	169	111	181	65
National Pride	164	117	194	80
Duty	152	93	158	66
Cultural Assimilation	150	69	217	100
Gender Parity	144	128	106	76
Obedience to Authority	132	83	170	91
Patriarchy	117	105	173	85

■ low (under 80)

▨ neutral (80–120)

▫ high (over 120)

ALERT READERS of the foregoing sections on community, personal
identity, and social organization will have noted that the lists of values
skewing Republican tend to be longer than those skewing Democratic.
This is not, as some partisans would claim, because Republicans have
cornered the market on values (after all, the values in our battery are a
mixed bag: a trend like *Acceptance of Violence* surely isn't what the "moral
values" voters were thinking of). But while they may not signal the
righteousness of one side and the vacuousness of the other, those lists are
an important sign.

REPUBLICANS

Republicans tend to have more extreme scores on more values—both
those they espouse and those they reject—because they're a relatively
coherent group. In their book *The Right Nation,* John Micklethwaite and
Adrian Wooldridge discuss how Republicans—libertarians and traditionalists, religious conservatives and business leaders, free-marketeers and
heartland true believers alike—have succeeded in keeping their troops
together despite their internal contradictions. Part of the Republicans'
success can be attributed to organization and discipline. And in keeping a
large, heterogeneous group from fratricide, a common enemy certainly
doesn't hurt either. During the Cold War, communism provided a ready
foe. Now the war on terror is the mission that unites diverse Republicans.
(Added glue is provided by the underdog mentality that has suffused the
current conservative movement, though the right's claims of marginality
and oppression by the "liberal elite" may prove a harder and harder sell as
Republican political dominance becomes ever more obvious.) But it's not
only party discipline and a common enemy that keeps them together. As
evidenced by the values profiles of the largest blocs of the Republican
coalition, they already share a great deal of common ground.

Democratic Party chairman and one-time presidential candidate
Howard Dean got himself into trouble in June of 2005 by remarking that
the Republican Party is "monolithic" and "pretty much a white, Christian
party." (Dean's Republican counterpart Ken Mehlman quipped that a lot

of people who attended his bar mitzvah would be surprised to learn that he leads a Christian party.) If he'd been going for the stereotypical trifecta, Dean could have added the word "rich" to his list: rich, white, Christian. Hyperbole aside, there is some truth to Dean's remarks.

Although it obviously isn't true that the Republican Party is made up *only* of white Christians, it *is* true that whites skew Republican; in the 2004 presidential election CNN's exit polls found that along with 44 percent of Latinos and just 11 percent of African Americans, 58 percent of white voters had voted Bush.

As for the Christian part, it's no secret that the Republican Party, particularly under born-again George W. Bush, has aggressively and successfully wooed the devoutly religious—especially evangelical Christians. Here again, exit polls found a correlation between Republican votes and both religion (59 percent of Protestants and 78 percent of evangelicals voted Bush) and religious service attendance (61 percent of those who attend church weekly voted Bush compared with 47 percent of those who attend a few times a year and 36 percent of those who never attend church).

Finally, despite all the populism of Republican messaging, the affluent do skew Republican and the less affluent Democrat. In 2004, among those earning less than $50K per year, 55 percent voted Kerry. Among those making more than $50K, 56 percent voted Bush, with the percentage increasing as the income brackets climbed.

So while the white, the religious, and the affluent aren't the only members of the Republican Party, these groups are clearly important pillars of support—and Republican messages need to connect with them effectively. Fortunately for the Republicans, the values of these three groups are not seriously at odds.[4]

To begin with, we find a fairly universal rejection of the hostile, Darwinist values of the lower-left quadrant. All three groups are weaker than average on the discriminatory trends *Xenophobia* and *Sexism,* and all three reject the value *Just Deserts,* which holds that those who meet with poverty or misfortune usually deserve their fate or have brought it on themselves. Moreover, these three groups are less likely than average to feel a general disconnection from or hostility to society. They report low levels of *Everyday Rage,* and are weak on the values *Anomie-Aimlessness* and *Civic Apathy.* In other words, white, affluent, and religious Americans are more likely than average to espouse values that signify engagement with and concern for their society.

All three of these groups are also more likely than average to believe that *Cultural Assimilation* is the best way for immigrants to integrate into American society. Although the religious considerably outstrip whites and affluent Americans in their belief in a strong *Work Ethic* and the attainability of the *American Dream,* each group is strong on both *Personal Control* and *Entrepreneurialism.* So while they vary somewhat in their beliefs about the equation between hard work and success, they all demonstrate an attachment to the idea of individual effort and achievement in the marketplace. (They're also above average in their enthusiasm for scientific progress, registered in their high scores on the value *Faith in Science.*)

The white, affluent, and religious further share a number of values that suggest moderate conservatism and traditionalism. Belief in traditional codes of behaviour is one: these Americans believe that people should do their duty even at the expense of their own happiness *(Duty);* they believe in good manners and appropriate dress in the name of not offending others *(Propriety);* and they believe in honesty and fair dealing in day-to-day life *(Everyday Ethics).*

On some traditional values the religious notably exceed the other two groups. They're stronger on the deferential trends *Obedience to Authority* and *National Pride;* they demonstrate a stronger attachment to the *Traditional Family;* and they're especially emphatic in their rejection of *Sexual Permissiveness.* White Americans are slightly above average on the trend *Traditional Family,* albeit not as ardent as the religious. But the affluent are stronger on *Flexible Families.*

The split between the religious and other important Republican constituencies evident in these values profiles is also apparent in Republican communications. A major challenge of the Bush White House, after all, has been to court religious supporters without alienating the party's more socially moderate members. When Republicans have championed measures to prevent same-sex marriages, for example, they've striven to appear not as bullies—angry men beating up on minority groups—but rather as moderates who are in *favour* of the traditional nuclear family. In this way, of course, they appeal to Americans' sense of *Duty* and *Propriety*, not prejudice. When Senator Rick Santorum suggested that homosexuality was just a step away from pedophilia, incest, and bestiality, he was rebuked by some moderate Republican senators and received no public support from the White House (to the chagrin of religious groups). Santorum is a Christian true believer who speaks his mind readily. More pragmatic Republican politicians tend to operate on the principle that it's possible to please most of the flock most of the time by speaking to the many values Republicans share and avoiding the (relatively few) values that divide them.

DEMOCRATS

The Democrats, by contrast, are relatively fragmented; factions in the Democratic coalition are more likely to disagree on values, counterbalance each other's scores, and thus bring the average Democratic score on any given value closer to the middle than the average Republican score. The Democratic base for most of the twentieth century consisted of liberal progressives, African Americans, Latinos, and organized labour. It's becoming increasingly difficult to appeal to all these disparate groups with a single message, and this is one reason for the Democrats' recent electoral woes. Anatol Lieven described the problem in the *London Review:*

> Democrat support ... is not so much a bloc as a congeries of interlocking clashes and dilemmas. The Democrats have somehow to reconcile the views and interests of the remnants of the unionised white working classes with those of blacks, of Latinos, of more progressive women and of a variety of cultural liberals. This isn't like herding cats: it's like trying to herd cats, dogs, and foxes all at once. Some of these groups don't just loathe each other culturally: they also have radically clashing economic interests.[5]

The values profiles of even certain-to-vote Democrats (a more coherent group than Democrats at large) point to this fragmentation: Democrats' indices on almost all trends are tepid because little consensus exists among the party's factions.

Upon signing the 1964 Civil Rights Act, President Lyndon Johnson famously said of the Democratic Party to an aide, "We have lost the South for a generation." He meant the white South, of course, and his prophecy continues to hold true today. The African Americans whose education, public services, and drinking fountains were declared no longer "separate but equal" under the act continue to overwhelmingly favour the Democratic Party. In 2004 African Americans voted Democrat by almost nine to one.

Latino Americans have also traditionally supported the Democratic Party, although this may be changing as they ascend the American socio-economic ladder and hold two identities—affluent and ethnic minority—that stereotypically conflict politically. Moreover, since strict Catholicism plays an important role in the lives of many American Latinos, Republican social conservatism may tend over time to attract them to the party. Nevertheless, most Latinos today still vote Democrat, and charged issues around Mexican labour and migration in border states—on which Republicans and Latinos tend to come down on opposing sides—may continue to drive a wedge between these Americans and the Republican Party.

Organized labour is, of course, another pillar of Democratic support. Antagonism between unions and free-market Republicans had its most famous recent example in 1981, when Ronald Reagan was faced with a nationwide air-traffic controller strike that threatened to wreak havoc on transportation. Reagan simply went ahead and fired all striking workers who failed to appear for work within a forty-eight-hour deadline. Union membership, and hence the ability of labour (self-identified as such) to mobilize politically, has been in decline for some time. But of those Americans who did live in union households in 2004, 59 percent voted Democrat.

A final pillar of Democratic support has long come from political progressives,[6] driven by values of equality, tolerance, and social justice.

Progressive priorities, of course, change over time (with progress). Since the twentieth century their central preoccupations have included socialist-leaning economic initiatives, equal rights for African Americans, feminism (from "votes for women" to "a woman's right to choose"), environmentalism, and most recently gay rights—not just the fight for same-sex marriage but for civil unions and legal protections against discrimination based on sexual orientation.

While we find relative coherence in the values of the key Republican subgroups, among these Democratic groups, common ground is scarcer real estate.

At one end of the spectrum, union members' values resemble those of socially moderate Republicans. They're strong on *Duty* and *Everyday Ethics*. They espouse similar optimism and enthusiasm for material progress, scoring high on the values *American Dream* and *Faith in Science*. In addition to their *Civic Engagement,* union members go out of their way to participate in their local communities, scoring high on *Community Involvement*. They register a fairly traditional outlook on matters of authority, scoring lower than average on *Equal Relationship with Youth*. And while African Americans register a similar level of community involvement, and progressives are just as politically engaged, on all the other values I've mentioned, union members stand apart from the other Democratic factions.

At the other end of the Democratic spectrum, in the lower-right quadrant of the map, political progressives are similarly isolated in their values. Such progressive priorities as *Ecological Concern* and *Ethical Consumerism* are simply off the radar for the other Democratic subgroups. On social issues, while union members share, somewhat tepidly, progressives' enthusiasm for *Gender Parity,* they drop off when it comes to diverse family models: progressives stand way out in their belief in *Flexible Families*. African Americans and Latinos are about average on *Flexible Families* and weaker than average on *Gender Parity,* both defining values for progressives. Some of their values emphasize a mode of engaging emotionally with the world that's notably absent among the other Democratic constituencies: progressives are alone in their embrace of *Introspection and*

Empathy and *Meaningful Moments,* for example. The one area of overlap between progressives and other Democratic groups relates to income redistribution: African Americans, Latinos, and union members all agree with progressives that, in general, the rich have some obligation to help the poor. Progressives and African Americans go further, reporting that they feel a personal obligation to help those worse off than themselves.

Although significant differences exist between the values of African Americans and Latinos, these two groups share more similarities than any other two subgroups that compose the Democratic coalition. Both groups have an above-average belief in *Patriarchy* and *Sexism* (compared with progressives' and union members' below-average scores). African Americans and Latinos also express greater than average disaffection with America's civic machinery; they're more likely than other Democratic factions to score high on *Civic Apathy.* On a more general level, both African Americans and Latinos score higher than average on the value *Fatalism.* They also have a longing for status and an enthusiasm for consumption that's absent among union members and political progressives: both African Americans and Latinos score above average on the values *Need for Status Recognition, Ostentatious Consumption,* and *Joy of Consumption.* African Americans score especially high on the value *Concern for Appearance,* while Latinos are about average. While *Xenophobia* is notably absent among all subgroups in the Democratic coalition, African Americans and Latinos are much more likely to actively espouse pluralism in matters of race and cultural practice: these two groups both score well above average on *Multiculturalism, Search for Roots,* and *Racial Fusion.* They enjoy only patchy agreement from progressives and union members on these values.

C LEARLY, A RELATIVELY SCATTERED PICTURE of the Democratic Party emerges when the values of its most important component groups are considered. Democrats tend to eschew most of the values at the upper extreme of the map that Republicans tend to embrace, but that's where the consensus ends. Republicans, by contrast, have a strong web of shared values that savvy candidates can leverage effectively. Republicans will inevitably disagree with each other as issues, personalities, and ideologies collide, but in the wake of policy disputes their shared values make it easier for them to reunite under some symbolically resonant banner. In a media-saturated age when sound bites and rapid-fire images are the main currency of a campaign, the fact that Republicans can more easily invoke symbols and language that are meaningful and appealing to the bulk of their likely supporters is an enormous advantage.

three

Gender and Race

Sometimes it's hard to be a woman.
—Tammy Wynette

The problem of the Twentieth Century is the problem of the color-line.
—W.E.B. Du Bois

IT'S BEEN SAID that there are two kinds of people in the world: those who believe the world can be divided into two kinds of people, and those who don't. As I describe the values of Americans, sometimes dividing them into a few piles according to ideology or engagement with their society, I suppose I reveal my basic faith in generalization.

One of the most famous and ardent generalizers of our day must be Harvard historian Samuel Huntington. Huntington is perhaps most famous for his 1996 book *The Clash of Civilizations and the New World Order* (expanded from a 1993 essay), which some saw as having predicted precisely the "new world order" that emerged in the wake of 9/11. Critics claimed at the time, however, that Huntington's model hopelessly over-simplified the situation, making monoliths out of mosaics.

Huntington had already replied to these criticisms in the preface to his book *The Soldier and the State,* published nearly forty years earlier. He claimed that generalizations were necessarily simplifications. And the job of those who study the world, he argued, is to make generalizations—to take the teeming experience of life, all the messy, unique facts of the world, and try to see patterns and commonalities. In short, to simplify. Don't just accuse me of simplifying, complained Huntington; come up with a better, truer generalization than the ones I offer.

Throughout most of this book, I generalize broadly about a society of over 300 million people, all unique. This approach naturally obscures important parts of the story of social change. I don't believe this fact invalidates my generalizations, but I do believe it's also worthwhile to examine subgroups within United States to nuance and enrich our understanding of how the society is changing. This chapter, then, will explore variations in social values and social change among Americans according to the demographics of gender and race; and the chapter that follows will explore those variations in relation to region.

GENDER

The 1999 movie *American Beauty* is ostensibly about one man's mid-life crisis. Frustrated professionally, personally, sexually, parentally, and domestically, Kevin Spacey's character begins to come apart at the seams. He exhibits mid-life crisis behaviour, some classic (buying a red sports car) and some not so classic (nearly sleeping with a friend of his daughter's for whom the age of consent is at least a birthday away). But to me, Annette Bening stole the show: her efforts to be a good mother, a successful businesswoman, and a sexual prize (initially to her husband and, later, to a slimy real estate colleague) are head-spinning.

The many demands placed on Bening's character beautifully converge in a scene in which she vacuums a carpet in a house she's about to try to sell, wearing just a slip (she doesn't want to get her suit dirty). As she vacuums—not as a homemaker, but as a businesswoman (somehow, she ends up vacuuming any way she slices it)—she repeats the motivational mantra "I will sell this house today! I will sell this house today!" She's stretched to the limit, and one senses that the mantra might be the only thing standing between her and meltdown. The slip is a wonderful touch: it conveys her sexuality (ignored until she develops a relationship with the obnoxious "king of real estate," who asks her in mid-coitus how she likes getting nailed by the king) even as her vacuuming reminds us that there's nothing sexual about her state of undress; it's a purely pragmatic response to a life in which she has too many roles to play in a day—she doesn't have time to change clothes as often as she changes hats.

In our surveys, we find that the values differences between American men and women in 2004 evoke, among other things, the stress under which women are working as they try to be June Cleaver to their kids, Pamela Anderson to their husbands, Oprah Winfrey to their friends, Martha Stewart to their guests, and Hillary Clinton to their colleagues at work. American women score higher than men on a number of anxiety-related values, foremost among them *Time Stress*. Driven by their above-average *Work Ethic,* they report that there's just too much to do in a day. This unease extends to the aids that ostensibly make life easier: women report higher *Technology Anxiety* than men, perhaps feeling they don't have time to keep up with what's supposed to save them time.

In the 1990s, manic motivator and fitness guru Susan Powter exhorted women to STOP THE INSANITY!! Women would love to; they outscore men on the values *Voluntary Simplicity* and *Personal Escape,* reporting that they're making special efforts to scale back their lives and take time out to escape the frenzy, if only behind their own eyelids for fifteen minutes. Women also report that they'd like to take more time to experience *Meaningful Moments* with others, not to mention exercise more and eat better. In light of women's longing to reduce stress and focus on what matters, it's little wonder that books like Richard Carlson's *Don't Sweat the Small Stuff (And It's All Small Stuff)* have flown off the shelves in the millions. Whether American women have found time to read them is another question.

Of course, life as an American man is not without its stresses. Work hours get longer and longer (fully five weeks a year more than in 1973, as I mentioned earlier). Commute times also lengthen as more Americans choose to live in exurbs where they can get the homes, schools, and security they desire. The U.S. Census Bureau reports that Americans spend over 100 hours a year commuting to work, and points out that this figure exceeds the two weeks (80 hours) of vacation time that many workers take over the course of a year. The average daily commute for Americans was 24.3 minutes in 2003, but those commuting in major cities take longer to get to and from work. And the proportion of Americans with mega-commutes (90 minutes or more—one way) is small but growing. Road rage is part and parcel of this experience, as only 5 percent of American commuters rely on public transport. So there's no question that men have their own increasingly gruelling daily grind, but it doesn't seem to be resulting in the same anxiety as we find among women.

Maybe it's the domestic labour that makes the difference. According to the University of Michigan's Institute for Social Research, as of 2002 American women spent an average of twenty-seven hours a week on housework, 60 percent more than men did. And while the amount of time women spend on housework has declined since 1985, this work is presumably being offloaded to a paid employee or simply neglected, as men's contribution to household labour has remained flat in that period.[1] Whether men are doing less work or just fewer kinds of work, their values reveal not only less anxiety and stress than women's profile suggests but also a distinct streak of confidence. Men feel sanguine about their ability to navigate a complex and fast-moving world (they score high on *Adaptive Navigation* and *Adaptability to Complexity*) and report high levels of confidence in society's collective march forward. They also express an above-average enthusiasm for new technology and a strong faith in scientific advances as a means of solving society's problems.

But however comfortable men may feel with complexity and change on the professional and technological front, they register a notable lack of enthusiasm for complexity and change in social matters: family, gender, and culture. Men considerably outscore women on the belief that "the father of the family must be master in his own house" *(Patriarchy)*, the belief that men are inherently superior to women *(Sexism)*, and the belief that it's inappropriate for individuals to dress or behave like members of the opposite sex *(Traditional Gender Identity)*. Men and women are more even in their views on the traditional family, but even here women are a little more open to diverse family models.

Women in general take a more flexible view of gender and family, believing less strongly that there's a single legitimate family model, that a family must be organized into a hierarchy with Dad as boss, and that gender roles are fixed, binary, and totally non-negotiable. We might imagine that moms are less likely than dads to lose sleep if their little boy wants to try on high heels or play at painting his nails one day or if their little girl squirms out of dresses because they hinder tree-climbing expeditions. By and large, the implications of stepping a little outside the gender box don't seem to alarm women as much as they do men.

"Sex brought us together, but gender drove us apart."

This flexibility among women extends to matters of culture as well; while men more strongly favour the idea that immigrants should make every effort to assimilate quickly into American culture, women are more likely to feel that America can be enriched by diverse cultural practices from around the world. Similarly, while men say they identify with and feel deeply attached to their own region, women are more likely to report that they feel like citizens of the world, at ease—at least imaginatively—with many ways of life. And women aren't more open to other cultures within and outside the United States because they're less patriotic; women outscore men on the value *National Pride.*

Speaking of *National Pride,* men and women each embrace some of the other authority-oriented trends located at the top of the map. The two groups seem to be attracted to different elements of the traditionalist world view, however. Men are more strongly focused on *Duty,* reporting that doing one's duty is more important than pursuing one's personal happiness. Among men's duties is to serve as family patriarch—which implies being not only the boss but also principal breadwinner and primary protector. In order to perform their duties as men, men must be, well, real men. Hence their emphasis on *Traditional Gender Identity.* The evangelical men's group the Promise Keepers offers perhaps the most distilled manifestation of this cluster of values. Advocating strong male leadership of the family and encouraging men to infuse their households with Christian "purity," the group insists in its literature that "real men matter."

Women, by contrast, tend to outscore men on traditional values related to community life and coexisting appropriately with others. For example, women are particularly strongly committed to honesty in their everyday dealings *(Everyday Ethics).* They're highly concerned with dressing and behaving in a manner appropriate to whatever occasion they encounter, and worry about offending others *(Propriety).*

Martha Stewart taps into many aspirations and longings in America, and one of them is American women's desire to do things *properly:* serving the right food on the right occasion; saying and doing the right things when guests arrive; making people comfortable by making them feel that things are naturally and easily under control. Stewart provides exhaustive instructions about endless domestic, cooking, gardening, and entertaining scenarios. Of course, she's often mocked for the comprehensiveness of her rules ("Now come on—she's telling us how to be tidier when we give the chinchillas a volcanic dust bath!"), but eliminating some of the question marks of family and social life is one of her most invaluable functions. No matter how obscure the question, Martha has a crisp, considered answer. Etiquette may be in decline in America, but as the saying goes, those who like it like it a lot. Martha helps them get it right.

Women's relatively greater interest in community life may well give rise to their idealistic streak. They outscore men on the value *Social Responsibility;* their concern for proper behaviour doesn't stop at providing guests with the perfect pilaf. It may also extend to providing strangers with some elements of a social safety net, even if only an ad hoc one. Panhandlers would go out of business if it weren't for the kindness of female strangers. Women also register greater interest than men do in *Ethical Consumerism* and *Ecological Concern.* Men may lead most of America's major charitable organizations, but women are their backbone and foot soldiers.

One last cluster of notable differentiating values: men are stronger than average on a number of trends in the lower-left quadrant, including *Acceptance of Violence, Everyday Rage, Xenophobia,* and *Just Deserts.* Now, the men driving these higher average scores are almost certainly not the same as those driving up their average score on such values as *Duty* and *Patriarchy* at the top of the map. Similarly, those driving up the average women's score on *Propriety* are likely not the same as those responsible for increasing women's average score on *Flexible Gender Identity.* The reason for these contradictory tendencies in both genders is age.

When we break down gender by age, as shown in the values map below, we see that men and women are distributed in an arc from the top-right *(Authenticity and Responsibility)* quadrant to the lower-left *(Exclusion and Intensity)* quadrant, with older Americans of both genders up and right and younger Americans down and left. It's clear that Americans' values are heavily informed by how old they are, with older Americans predictably espousing more traditional values. But gender also exerts an influence that appears constant across age cohorts: women are generally farther right than men are, espousing values more strongly associated with fulfillment. Three female segments fall into the

Authenticity and Responsibility quadrant; no male segments do. This difference is consistent with women's higher overall scores on introspective trends such as *Spiritual Quest* and *Meaningful Moments*. It's also consistent not only with men's higher scores on the hard-edged Darwinist trends at the extreme left of the map, but also with the more productively individualistic trends around the middle of the map, such as *Entrepreneurialism* and *Adaptability to Complexity*.

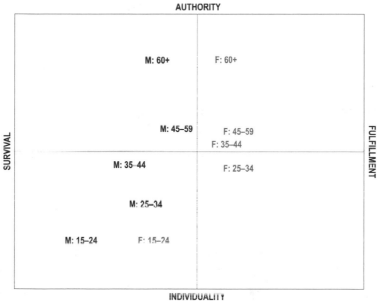

Combined Data, 1992, 1996, 2000, 2004

To date, the gaps between men and women on the values map have remained fairly constant. That is, men and women over the age of sixty are not much farther apart than are men and women between the ages of fifteen and twenty-four. This is not a little surprising, since most would probably agree that American men's and women's economic, educational, and professional opportunities, as well as their lifestyles, have converged considerably in the last half-century. As time passes, it will be interesting to observe whether men's and women's values do finally begin to converge or whether the still murky mix of biology and cultural norms that constitute gender will conspire to maintain (or even increase?) that stubborn gap between the values of America's boys and girls.

RACE

W.E.B. Du Bois's famous remark at the opening of this chapter is perhaps the most often quoted declaration about race in America. He wrote these words in his 1903 treatise *The Souls of Black Folk,* and when we look back on them from the other side of the century, it's certainly hard to dispute their prescience.

But important as the line between black and white has been to the unfolding of American history since the slave trade began in the mid seventeenth century, it's harder in the twenty-first century than it was in the twentieth to speak meaningfully of a single colour line. This isn't to say that race is no longer a powerful force in American society. But internal social change and migration have meant that the old line between white/free/European and black/slave/African is only part of the picture of race in America. The twentieth century saw not only growth in other non-European populations in America (Latino,[2] South Asian, and East Asian) but also greater integration among racial groups—both socially and in the more intimate form of intermarriage.

In July 2004 the Census Bureau found Hispanics to account for 14.1 percent of the U.S. population. And with their high fertility rates and continued immigration from Mexico and elsewhere, Hispanics are the fastest-growing group in American society. Samuel Huntington writes in his 2004 book *Who Are We?* that America's identity is threatened by its burgeoning Latino population. One may disagree with Huntington's perspective, but the information he offers about the sheer size of America's Latino population is undoubtedly important. If desegregation and efforts toward racial justice for blacks were the crucial racial matters of the twentieth century (this project is far from complete, but there's no question that much progress has been made), the manner in which America both absorbs and influences its large and growing Latino population may well be the dominant "racial" issue in the twenty-first.

The ideal of America as melting pot, a place that receives and assimilates immigrants from around the world, has been much questioned. Some see the melting pot as a worthy goal that America falls short of achieving. Others reject the ideal altogether in favour of a more deliberately pluralist society. Meanwhile, our data indicate that Americans of the three most populous racial groups are sharing more and more values, suggesting that, remarkably, the melting pot may indeed still be blurping away.

But first a word on our method. In our profiles of racial groups we combined the data from all four survey waves, thereby increasing our sample sizes and providing more robust conclusions. The drawback, however, is that combining the waves obscures change over time. So how can I say that the three racial groups we profile here are becoming more similar if our analysis doesn't permit us to see how they're changing over time? Because of generational differences in values: the younger members of all three groups are vastly more similar to one another than are the older members. Black, white, and Latino youth whose grandparents' values are very dissimilar could sit down together and agree on a host of issues. The consensus they'd reach wouldn't necessarily please any of their grandparents, but it would be consensus nevertheless. I'll first look at the values of older members of America's three largest racial groups, and then describe the youth segments, which share considerably more common ground.

African Americans over Age Sixty

There are four main strains of values that best differentiate older African Americans from older whites and Latinos. These are a communitarian quest for fulfillment, a strong belief in pluralism, a longing for status (and the ability to display status materially), and frustrated disengagement.

In their search for personal fulfillment, older African Americans register interest both in a *Spiritual Quest* and in seeking meaning from family and community. While older African Americans, whites, and Latinos all register above-average attachment to religion, African Americans are particular in their personal and introspective approach to spiritual practice.

They're stronger than their white and Latino age peers on both *Primacy of the Family* and *Community Involvement*. African Americans are more likely than others to say they've attended a meeting or rally on a topic of concern to their neighbourhood or city, and more likely to report that they identify with people who put their family ahead of everything else. Interestingly, older African Americans are much *weaker* than their white and Latino age peers on the trend *Civic Engagement,* suggesting that although they feel powerfully connected to their neighbours and local communities, they feel relatively little attachment to larger social institutions that would ask them to vote or serve on a jury.

Older African Americans are strong on *Search for Roots* and *Multiculturalism* and weak on *Cultural Assimilation*. They believe that "America would be a better place if ethnic and racial groups maintained their cultural identities." On a personal level, they're more likely than their white and Latino age peers to agree that "It's important for me to feel connected to my cultural roots."

They're also stronger than their age peers on *Need for Status Recognition* and on a number of status-by-consumption trends, including *Ostentatious Consumption* and *Importance of Brand*. This quest for status isn't merely about wealth; for example, older African Americans score high on *Concern for Appearance,* which emphasizes not necessarily looking wealthy but rather appearing appropriate and well groomed.

And while this segment also scores high on *Work Ethic,* suggesting a willingness to work hard to achieve longed-for status, older African Americans score low on *American Dream*. This finding suggests that by and large they don't believe that with hard work anyone can truly make it in America. And it's perhaps this disillusionment that gives rise to the *Fatalism* we see in this segment, the sense of *Anomie-Aimlessness,* and even the frustration in the form of *Everyday Rage*.

White Americans over Age Sixty

Older white Americans diverge from their African-American and Latino age peers on four main fronts: their traditionalism (including patriotism), their relative lack of interest in consumption, their rejection of pluralism, and their civic engagement. One could argue that with the exception of consumption-related values, the values that differentiate older white Americans from their African-American and Latino age peers largely revolve around their greater sense of belonging to and being represented by America and its institutions.

First, the traditionalism of this group gives rise to an old-fashioned patriotism: they're especially strong on the trend *National Pride,* reporting that being American is part of their personal identity and that it's important to them that America hold a strong position in the world. They also demonstrate above-average commitment to the *Traditional Family* and reject other family models, such as common-law, same-sex, and single-parent families. They're especially likely to register a strong sense of *Duty*— which for these Americans surely applies to both family and country.

Speaking of country, their vision of America, while tolerant, is assimilationist and not especially flexible. Older white Americans aren't particularly strong on *Xenophobia,* but they are strong on *Cultural Assimilation.* In other words, they don't mind immigrants as long as they're willing to hurry up and "become American" so they can start pursuing the same American Dream as everyone else. Moreover, although not hostile to people of other backgrounds, older white Americans are not enthused about racial mixing *(Racial Fusion)* or having a diverse group of friends and partaking in traditions from elsewhere in the world *(Culture Sampling).*

Older white Americans score somewhat higher than their Latino age peers and vastly higher than their African-American age peers on the value *Civic Engagement,* suggesting that these Americans feel a greater stake in and connection to American politics.

Finally, they're distinguished from their age peers of other races by their relative lack of interest in consumption: they're weak on *Joy of Consumption, Buying on Impulse, Confidence in Advertising,* and *Ostentatious Consumption.*

LATINO AMERICANS OVER AGE SIXTY

Older Latino Americans hold some traditional values strongly, but not the same ones as older white Americans. While the latter group emphasizes duty and patriotism, older Latinos score higher on the more personal traditional values of *Religiosity* and *Everyday Ethics*.

Like older African Americans, who emphasize family and community so heavily, older Latinos score well above average on *Primacy of the Family*. They score especially high on the value *Celebrating Passages*, suggesting a longing to observe and celebrate milestones in their own lives and in the lives of those close to them, likely milestones rooted in their *Religiosity*: first communions, confirmations, and weddings.

Latino Americans over the age of sixty also score above average on a number of introspective and fulfillment-oriented trends, including *Introspection and Empathy* and *Effort Toward Health*. In keeping with this relatively inner-directed orientation, they register very little interest in consumption; they outscore their age peers on *Brand Apathy* and are disinclined to trust advertisers' messages.

Although they're engaged with their families and communities and take comfort from their religious faith, older Latino Americans register some anxiety about the pace of change in the world around them. They're uneasy with some technological developments, scoring high on *Technology Anxiety*, and concerned about the privacy violations these new technologies might engender. They're uncomfortable about change and complexity in a more general sense as well, outscoring their age peers on *Aversion to Complexity*.

Young Americans: Black, White, Latino

Most of the differences we perceive among older people of different races in the United States disappear when we look at the values of youth. In Chapter 1 we saw the average position of all Americans drifting into the lower-left *Exclusion and Intensity* quadrant of the social values map. American youth of all three races are deep in the lower-left corner of this quadrant; their profiles are overwhelmingly similar. But whereas the older members of these three groups all articulate some vision of community and personal fulfillment, youth of all backgrounds are intent on the values of the lower-left quadrant: thrills, consumption, and Darwinism.

In short, youth are for the most part embracing the values driving many Americans' evolution into the *Exclusion and Intensity* quadrant. Whites, Latinos, and African Americans under the age of twenty all score well above average on the full slate of Darwinist values: *Acceptance of Violence, Civic Apathy, Everyday Rage, Anomie-Aimlessness, Sexism, Ecological Fatalism,* and *Just Deserts.* Similar consensus resounds on thrill-seeking values: *Penchant for Risk, Pursuit of Intensity, Attraction for Crowds,* and *Living Virtually.* And the story is the same for consumption: if you've got it, flaunt it. White, Latino, and African-American youth are all well above average on *Joy of Consumption, Ostentatious Consumption, Buying on Impulse,* and *Advertising as Stimulus.*

This embrace of *Exclusion and Intensity* values is one side of the coin; the other side is the rejection of both authority- and fulfillment-oriented trends at the top and right of the map. Youth of all backgrounds are vastly below average on *Duty, National Pride, Primacy of the Family, Traditional Family, Religiosity,* and *Propriety.* They are similarly left cold by the quaint *Everyday Ethics* and *Introspection and Empathy. Gender Parity* and *Ecological Concern* are also outside these young people's scheme of priorities.

When progressives of the past dreamed of young Americans walking hand in hand in a colour-blind society, surely this was not the consensus they envisioned.

four

Region

We always refer to ourselves as real America.
Rural America, real America, real, real America.
—Dan Quayle, remarking on his Indiana roots

IN THE WEEKS FOLLOWING the 2004 presidential election, electoral maps began to circulate on the internet. There had been maps before then, of course, especially on election night. Or rather, there had been one map: the famous colour-coded one, born in 2000. This map took the colours red and blue and piled them (accurately or not) with political, cultural, religious, and emotional meaning until they groaned under the weight. But after the election, ordinary Americans who had spent the evening of November 2 glued to that single televised map began to think more critically about the image, and began to produce their own variations.

For triumphant Republicans, post-election mapmaking involved shading not just states but counties according to their vote. Rural areas of blue states quickly reddened; the swath of red through the heartland came to appear even more impressive, and the (now patchy) blue coasts appeared even more marginal. For depressed Democrats, the mapmaking process involved finding ways to represent the size of the population in blue states—to show that the relative slivers of blue space on the map were chock full of people while the vast red middle was, in many places, more brush than Bush.

Much of this exercise, of course, was merely a graphic articulation of a political squabble: Americans, win or lose, were seeking legitimacy for their own political views by showing how many people shared them. But they could have done that with numbers. What the maps did was overlay—however simplistically—regional identities onto the political debate.

The rhetoric of the "heartland," so beloved of the Bush administration, of course positions the red middle of the country as the heart of America, rendering the liberal coasts useful, but ultimately inessential, extremities. The maps of both sides, designed to have the favoured colour occupy as much space as possible, sought to position Republican or Democratic views as not just held by more Americans but as being literally more American by constituting more, (geo)graphically, of America.

Americans of every region can argue for their own region's status as the most quintessentially American. New Englanders live in the cradle of the Union. Midwesterners live, literally, in Middle America; one of them (Bob? Carol?) must surely be the famed but so far anonymous Average American. Those on the West Coast inhabit the perpetual frontier, the land of the American Dream, the place to which every American settler aspired even if he or she didn't know it. Those in the South are twice American: old-fashioned U.S.A. writ large—ranches, guns, pickup trucks, open spaces, and all the freedom a man can handle (and then some, in a few cases)—and growing cities like Atlanta and Austin that attest to the region's energy, entrepreneurialism, and ambition.

Although the electoral maps with their colour binary certainly obscure a lot about America's regions, they speak to the desire to show the place where one lives affirmed in its Americanness by being in step with the rest of the country: "Where I live, people voted Bush/Kerry; and look how many other Americans think the way we do." America, despite or perhaps because of its diversity, has a long tradition of dividing itself into poles. North versus South was of course the most acrimonious division, from the Civil War to civil rights. East versus West was more a cultural than a political division—the established (some would say establishment) East and the untamed, individualistic West. Now the red-and-blue map of the so-called 50–50 nation offers another binary that will die hard: middle versus coasts (and embedded in that division, rural versus urban).

When we develop values profiles of America's regions, the portraits that emerge contain elements of all these identities as well as other local particularities wrought by climate, history, ethnocultural composition, density, and economics.[1]

MOUNTAIN

The Mountain[2] region's values reveal a bastion of individualism consistent with the stereotype of the Montana loner: a stereotype that ranges from the truly anti-social—in the manner of Unabomber Ted Kaczynski, who lived in a cabin outside Lincoln, Montana—to the rugged but productive and presumably housetrained Marlboro Man. Mountain residents on average reject many forms of traditional authority and register considerable confidence in their ability to negotiate change and complexity. There's an idealistic streak in this region, but a marked ambivalence about which of society's institutions are most effective in realizing the region's ideals.

Residents of the Mountain region are weak on most of the deferential trends at the top of the map. They register relatively little interest in *Religiosity,* and they report little attachment to a sense of *Duty* that might compel them to defer to authority (or to practise *Everyday Ethics,* on which they're the weakest of any region). Rather, this region is among the stronger ones on *Rejection of Authority.* In keeping with their aversion to hierarchy, these Americans also score high on the value *Equal Relationship with Youth.* Ideologically, Mountain men and women are more libertarian than social or religious conservative.

One prominent exception to this rule is Colorado Springs, where Reverend James Dobson established the base of his powerful Focus on the

Family organization. Since this religious lobby group put down roots in Colorado Springs, the once sleepy town has become a major hub of Christian conservative activity. Then again, just a short drive away is the hippie enclave of Boulder, where a resident told me only half-jokingly that the biggest religious conflict in recent memory was a spat between competing Buddhist sects. If Colorado Springs is a little patch of the Deep South at higher altitude, Boulder is a cross between New England and Seattle. Every region has its idiosyncrasies.

On average, the values of Mountain region residents suggest they feel little anxiety about the changes taking place around them: weak on *Aversion to Complexity*, these Americans feel confident in their ability to make decisions effectively in the absence of dictates from institutions and authority figures. And they may be relatively weak on *Religiosity*, but they're notably strong on *Spiritual Quest*—an apparent contradiction that points to an interest in seeking fulfillment without having their spiritual practice dictated by other people or by tradition.

Mountain region dwellers are also strong on *Flexible Families;* they feel that individuals should be able to construct their families as they see fit, without condemnation or, more important, interference from others. These individualists are also weak on the trend *Traditional Gender Identity,* demonstrating that they resist strict codes of behaviour, whether imposed by authority figures like religious leaders or merely absorbed through social convention.

One interesting contradiction that emerged in Montana in the wake of the 2004 election nicely crystallizes the Mountain region's commitment to individualism, which can lead both to predictable conservatism and to less intuitive policy outcomes. In 2004, the state voted to re-elect George W. Bush and also voted to legalize medical marijuana. Montanans liked Republican freedom rhetoric, but liked it so much they declared themselves free to deviate from the party line. The Marlboro Man is dying of cancer, and no politician is going to tell him he can't have a little toke if it eases his exit from this rock-strewn world.

In light of this region's individualism, it's not surprising that its residents express little enthusiasm for status-seeking through consumption. This segment is weak on *Ostentatious Consumption* and takes scant pleasure from spending money on new possessions *(Joy of Consumption)*—which may flow in part from its relative uninterest (or perhaps loss of faith) in the *American Dream*. Since these people are less likely than the average American to equate material success with personal merit, for them the ostentatious display of wealth primarily signals a need to impress.

Residents of the Mountain region register little anxiety about their day-to-day lives. This segment is weak on *Everyday Rage* as well as *Time Stress*. Since its values profile signals equanimity about life (including comfort with change and complexity and stress levels that aren't excessive), it follows that there's little reflexive anger here toward social "others": these Americans are weak on *Xenophobia*.

Although this region is also weak on trends associated with deference to religious organizations and traditional authority structures, there's a certain confidence here in both business and political institutions. Mountain residents express enthusiasm for *Active Government* and faith in both the political process and the private sector as mechanisms for bettering society. It may seem strange that such ardent individualists would have such faith in their government. One possible explanation may be that, as Walter Kirn noted in *The New York Times Magazine,* Westerners have proven very astute in enacting legislative expressions of popular will (as in the case of legalized medical marijuana), even when political barriers are in the way. Kirn brands this behaviour "vigilante democracy." But this segment's belief in *Active Government* (the idea that government can be, *pace* Ronald Reagan, part of the solution and not part of the problem) should not be mistaken for socialist sentiment. There's little enthusiasm in the individualistic Mountain region for a general ethos of wealth redistribution: this group is weak on the values *Largesse Oblige* and *Social Responsibility*.

Mountain Values Profile

Strongest		Weakest	
Rejection of Authority	121	Religiosity	78
Equal Relationship with Youth	120	Aversion to Complexity	57
Spiritual Quest	127	Traditional Gender Identity	72
Flexible Families	137	Ostentatious Consumption	79
Active Government	124	Joy of Consumption	78
More Power for Politics	154	American Dream	71
More Power for Business	133	Xenophobia	77
		Largesse Oblige	77
		Social Responsibility	62

■ low (under 80)

▨ neutral (80–120)

▫ high (over 120)

MID-ATLANTIC

Compared with other regions, the Mid-Atlantic[3] is individualistic and survival oriented. Its residents tend to register a willingness to defer to political, but not moral, authority figures.

Mid-Atlantic dwellers are more likely than other Americans to feel disconnected from society. They're weak on many of the key authority-oriented trends on the map, including *Religiosity, Obedience to Authority,* and *Patriarchy.* These low scores indicate that they not only reject the authority of religious leaders and traditional family patriarchs but question the whole category of the authority figure. It makes sense, then, that these Americans are strong on the trend *Equal Relationship with Youth* at the bottom of the map. In a more traditional and hierarchical world view, youth must defer to elders because authority accrues through age; whereas for those who are suspicious of authority, youth should be treated as equals unless they demonstrate otherwise through their personal behaviour. Finally, the moralism often associated with authority has a weak grip on this segment, which is tied for the highest score on the value *Sexual Permissiveness*.

Mid-Atlantic residents may score low on the more traditional value *Religiosity*, but they score even lower on the more personal fulfillment–oriented *Spiritual Quest*, suggesting that they're not much interested in pursuing spiritual fulfillment by their own lights either.

And this apathy extends into other areas of life: these Americans are stronger than average on *Civic Apathy*, suggesting they feel they can have little influence as political agents and don't care to try. They're also stronger than residents of other regions on the trends *Fatalism* and *Anomie-Aimlessness*. Their *Fatalism* suggests that they feel they have little control over the way their lives unfold and that destiny will take its course regardless of their actions, and their high score on *Anomie-Aimlessness* indicates a sense of personal aimlessness and disengagement from society. So it follows that they're also less likely than other Americans to feel part of the global village: Mid-Atlantic residents are strong on the trend *Parochialism*, which measures one's sense of disconnectedness from the world beyond one's immediate surroundings.

It's noteworthy that although Mid-Atlantic residents reject traditional authority, they exhibit a certain paternalist tendency in their high scores on *Active Government* and *More Power for Politics*. It stands to reason that they believe some power—in this case governmental power—should intervene to help individuals, since in their fatalistic world view individuals are fairly powerless to alter their own circumstances.

Unsurprisingly in view of their fatalism, Mid-Atlantic residents are weak on both *American Dream* and *Entrepreneurialism*. Nevertheless, they report that they're consuming images of the Dream with increasing regularity, watching more television and paying more attention to celebrities. We label this value *Living Virtually*. The Mid-Atlantic *Enthusiasm for New Technology* is underpinned by two things: a desire to connect to the world of entertainment and celebrity in new ways and a wish to signify affluence with the possession of new gadgets. Mid-Atlantic residents, strong on *Concern for Appearance*, pay a great deal of attention to the image they present to the world. They're also weak on

Discriminating Consumerism; Mid-Atlantic residents are willing to buy on impulse, seduced by the promises of marketers and their wares rich in cultural meaning.

The Mid-Atlantic is the strongest region on *Acceptance of Violence,* a logical corollary, perhaps, to this region's anxiety about impressing others and to its feeling of disconnectedness from society. After all, one of the items that constitute this trend asks respondents to agree or disagree that "It's acceptable to use physical force to get something you really want. The important thing is to get what you want." When the desire for the "something" is intensified and the concern for others who may be barriers to its acquisition is diminished, it's easier to agree with a statement such as this.

Mid-Atlantic Values Profile

Strongest		Weakest	
Equal Relationship with Youth	121	Religiosity	79
Sexual Permissiveness	130	Obedience to Authority	83
Civic Apathy	124	Patriarchy	78
Fatalism	140	Spiritual Quest	67
Anomie-Aimlessness	120	American Dream	88
Parochialism	124	Entrepreneurialism	85
Active Government	144	Discriminating Consumerism	81
More Power for Politics	150		
Living Virtually	141		
Enthusiasm for New Technology	130		
Concern for Appearance	115		
Acceptance of Violence	128		

low (under 80)

neutral (80–120)

high (over 120)

DEEP SOUTH

In 1963 Flannery O'Connor wrote, "Whenever I am asked why Southern writers particularly have this penchant for writing about freaks, I say it is because we are still able to recognize one." The Deep South[4] stands out as the most religious, socially conservative, and rigidly traditional region in the United States. This is a population deeply attached to authority and to the religious, national, and familial rules that authority figures dictate. Running afoul of these rules might make you a freak in some parts of the Deep South even today, whereas in other parts of America, adhering to them might be an equally eccentric choice.

Residents of the Deep South are profoundly deferential to traditional authority: theirs is the single strongest region on the trends *Religiosity* and *Patriarchy*. The pastors and fathers to whom these Americans defer help each other instill an ardent belief in the *Primacy of the Family* and in the *Traditional Family* as the only legitimate family model.

To these Americans it's self-evident that family, like society, should be organized hierarchically, with the father as the undisputed head of the household. They not only reject *Heterarchy* (the idea that groups can be effectively organized with flat and fluid leadership structures) but are strong on the trend *Sexism,* being more likely than other Americans to believe that men and women have different inherent characteristics and that men are naturally and essentially superior. They believe gender identity is immutable, strongly rejecting the idea of *Flexible Gender Identity*.

Deep South residents also feel a strong patriotic deference to America; they have the highest score of all U.S. regions on the trend *National Pride.* This is perhaps an unexpected outcome for a region that wanted to secede just 150 years ago, but Southerners remain interested both in their American identity and their personal connections with their own beloved region and its history *(Search for Roots)*.

In sum, the emphasis we find in the Deep South on family, religion, region, and nation suggests that these Americans see their personal identities as heavily bound up in the institutions to which they belong.

Adherence to the codes of these institutions is the primary way in which Deep South residents express their sense of personal responsibility and achievement. (This region scores low on several trends associated with personal well-being divorced from external institutions, including *Personal Escape* and *Holistic Health*.) In the values profile of the Deep South, then, moralism trumps individualism.

There's a clear streak of fearfulness and anxiety in the values profile of the Deep South. As this region sees its traditional values losing hold in some quarters of American society, it clings to them all the more fiercely. These Americans are relatively uncomfortable with complexity and rapid change *(Aversion to Complexity)*. The flexibility, mixing, and hybridity that characterize so much of life in contemporary American society makes many Deep South residents particularly uncomfortable; they score especially low on *Racial Fusion, Religion à la Carte*, and *Culture Sampling*—all trends that imply the mixing of disparate people, ideas, and practices.

This anxiety about change isn't merely an abstract distaste for multiculturalism or "moral relativism"; Deep South residents register fear about actual violations of their privacy and safety. Unease about possible encroachments on personal privacy, likely facilitated by technological change, is high in this region *(Protection of Privacy)*. As well, they're more likely than all other Americans to fear violence in their daily lives *(Fear of Violence)*. Finally, in their fear of outsiders of other cultures and races, the Deep South is matched only by the Texarkana region in *Xenophobia*.

These Americans are clinging to the rules and institutions that imposed order on society in what many Southerners see as a simpler, safer, saner past. And the more these institutions are flouted by the population at large, the more there is to be angry about: the Deep South is among the strongest segments on the trend *Everyday Rage*. Many Southerners must have been able to relate when William F. Buckley launched the conservative *National Review* and wrote that its purpose was to stand athwart history yelling "Stop!"

Deep South Values Profile

Strongest		Weakest	
Religiosity	146	Heterarchy	78
Patriarchy	153	Flexible Gender Identity	78
Traditional Family	165	Personal Escape	77
Primacy of the Family	120	Holistic Health	62
Sexism	125	Racial Fusion	73
National Pride	134	Religion à la Carte	71
Search for Roots	120	Culture Sampling	67
Aversion to Complexity	121		
Voluntary Simplicity	122		
Protection of Privacy	144		
Fear of Violence	127		
Everyday Rage	120		
Xenophobia	124		

low (under 80)

neutral (80–120)

high (over 120)

MIDWEST

The values that most distinguish the Midwest[5] from the other regions of the United States can be understood in relation to a single concept: conformity. But while this orientation is profound, it's not the traditional, religious, small-town conformity of the familiar stereotype.

The Midwest is the strongest of all the American regions on the trend *Cultural Assimilation*. Midwesterners believe that immigrants should leave the customs and cultures of their nations of origin behind and actively integrate into American culture. And they favour this cultural conformity not only for others but for themselves as well: weak on *Search for Roots*, these Americans demonstrate little interest in exploring the particularities of their own history and lineage, and are equally unenthused about preserving the distinctiveness of their region's identity. They're happy with the anglicized names many of their forebears accepted from immigration officials on Ellis Island; they're not about to make waves by rediscovering or "reclaiming" historical characteristics that make them different from their neighbours. They're also among the weakest Americans on the trend *Culture Sampling*. Given their minimal interest in diverse foods, traditions, and ideas from around the world, it follows that they wouldn't feel a pressing need to foster a microcosm of that diversity at home.

Midwesterners are weaker than average on many of the trends associated with self-knowledge and personal exploration. For example, this region is among the weakest on both *Spiritual Quest* and *Religion à la Carte*. These Americans aren't drawn to seeking meaning through an individual quest for spiritual fulfillment or to exploring diverse religions and choosing elements they find compelling. A personalized approach to spiritual practice does not sit well with Midwesterners, who don't want to stand out.

Even a health-related trend with an inner-directed bent is of little interest. Weak on the trend *Holistic Health*, Midwesterners would rather not spend time exploring the links between their physical and psychic well-being; their bodies, like their cars, should work. If they don't, they should be fixed or medicated.

But if their values register little interest in exploring personal, cultural, or spiritual particularities, to what are these Americans conforming? Contrary to the stereotype of the Midwest as religious, family-oriented Middle America, we find no particular emphasis on religion, family, or traditional social mores here. Midwesterners are relatively weak on both *Propriety* and *Primacy of the Family*. And while they don't emphatically reject authority (they're weak on *Rejection of Authority* and espouse none of the rebellious trends in the lower-left quadrant), they're not especially compelled by old-fashioned "family values." They're not particularly intent on using old-fashioned hard work to climb the ladder of American success, for one thing. They are, in fact, the weakest of all the regions on *Work Ethic*, an ethos that has been eroded along with many of the industries in the rust belt that was once America's industrial heartland.

Midwestern conformity seems to revolve not around moralism but around consumption. Although ostentation does not come through strongly in their values profile, these Americans are interested in sending the right signals to others by owning the right brands. They take cues on how to stay centred in the mainstream by paying attention to entertainment media and celebrities (they score above average on the value *Living Virtually*). Though skeptical of political institutions and processes (they're weak on *More Power for Politics*), they have considerable confidence in those who've experienced success in the American marketplace (they have high *Confidence in Big Business*).

It's noteworthy that Midwesterners are the third strongest regional segment on the trend *Everyday Rage*. Eschewing personal quests for fulfillment and no longer strongly attached to traditional sources of meaning, Midwesterners appear to have a deep and grinding feeling of dissatisfaction that manifests itself as anger in day-to-day situations.

Midwest Values Profile

Strongest		Weakest	
Cultural Assimilation	127	Search for Roots	81
Importance of Brand	115	Culture Sampling	73
Living Virtually	117	Spiritual Quest	75
Confidence in Big Business	111	Religion à la Carte	82
Everyday Rage	121	Personal Creativity	76
		Holistic Health	88
		Propriety	68
		Primacy of the Family	82
		Rejection of Authority	80
		Work Ethic	59
		More Power for Politics	79
		Social Responsibility	85

■ low (under 80)

■ neutral (80–120)

□ high (over 120)

NEW ENGLAND

New Englanders[6] are the most autonomy- and fulfillment-oriented group in the United States. They're the most likely to reject the dictates of authority figures and strive instead toward a fulfillment they define for themselves. A strong communitarian streak also marks this oldest region of America; residents of New England are more intent than any other Americans on community involvement—apparently affirming Senator Barak Obama's insistence at the 2004 Democratic National Convention that "We coach Little League in the blue states."

These residents are considerably more likely than others to embrace the trend *Rejection of Authority:* they believe that individuals can and should make choices about all areas of their lives, unfettered by deference to religious leaders, superiors at work, or the family patriarch. And their scores on other trends bear this out. New Englanders are weaker than most others on *Religiosity,* rejecting the authority of religious leaders to prescribe and enforce an entire way of life. Rather, they believe in their own ability to autonomously select aspects of various faiths and traditions that are meaningful to them personally; hence, their high scores on *Religion à la Carte.*

Also consistent with their *Rejection of Authority,* they're the most likely of all Americans to reject the adage that "the father of the family must be master in his own house." Not only do they believe in a more fluid and egalitarian distribution of power within the family, but they're more willing than most to question the idea that the traditional family (two married parents of the opposite sex and their biological children) is the only legitimate one. New England is the strongest of all the regions on the trend *Flexible Families.*

Further, these Americans are among the weakest on the trend *National Pride,* making them more likely than most to question the authority of institutions and abstractions and less likely than most to feel strong patriotic attachment or to wish to demonstrate the superiority or dominance of their country to citizens of other nations. (Their high score on *More Power for Media* may well reflect a belief that the media should hold government to account for its actions and function as a proxy for informed and skeptical citizens.)

"Sure, we have common ground with Middle America—
we're all carbon-based life forms."

This rejection of authority among New Englanders dovetails with a more generalized *Rejection of Order*. Their high score on this value indicates that they don't place great importance on adhering to strict schedules, having meticulously organized homes, or otherwise exerting strong control over their environment. On the level of personal identity, this rejection of order manifests itself as a willingness to question the conventional gender binary: New Englanders are more likely than most to feel comfortable manifesting both masculine and feminine characteristics (they score low on the value *Traditional Gender Identity*). They're also less likely than other Americans to espouse values (such as *Sexism* and *Xenophobia*) that register hostility to social "others."

Residents of New England manifest relatively little interest in impressing people: they have low scores on both *Need for Status Recognition* and *Look Good Feel Good* (a trend that measures the extent to which people's personal appearance affects their sense of well-being). It's their focus on autonomy and personal fulfillment (as opposed to ostentation) that underpins their lack of interest in consumption—particularly conspicuous consumption. These Americans are predictably weak on *Ostentatious Consumption* and *Importance of Brand.*

New Englanders are particularly skeptical of advertising, having little faith in its promises and rarely taking pleasure from using it as a stimulus to consumption *(Advertising as Stimulus).* This skepticism flows from their leeriness not only of consumption in general but of the motives and methods of business; they're weak on both *Confidence in Big Business* and *Confidence in Small Business.*

New England Values Profile

Strongest		Weakest	
Rejection of Authority	126	Patriarchy	33
Religion à la Carte	131	Religiosity	70
Flexible Families	147	National Pride	73
More Power for Media	124	Traditional Gender Identity	72
Rejection of Order	130	Sexism	62
Community Involvement	125	Xenophobia	64
Civic Engagement	120	Need for Status Recognition	74
		Look Good Feel Good	58
		Ostentatious Consumption	74
		Importance of Brand	79
		Advertising as Stimulus	77
		Confidence in Advertising	77
		Confidence in Big Business	53
		Confidence in Small Business	71

■ low (under 80)

▦ neutral (80–120)

▫ high (over 120)

A final distinguishing characteristic is New Englanders' emphasis on both *Community Involvement* and *Civic Engagement*. They are, in fact, considerably stronger on these trends than are Americans in any other region. Their belief in autonomy should not therefore be confused with a belief in untrammelled individualism; their cooperative and egalitarian vision of community is consistent with their skepticism of top-down social organization.

PACIFIC

The values profile of the Pacific[7] region reveals an interesting blend of two popular images of America's West Coast, and particularly of California: the individualist seeking adventure and new experience, and the countercultural pilgrim seeking understanding and fulfillment. Just as traditionalism can at its edges turn to bigotry in more conservative regions, the quest for freedom from authority and tradition can at its edges turn to nihilism in the Pacific region.

In keeping with the individualism so often associated with the West Coast, the endpoint of the American frontier, this region is the strongest in America on the trend *Rejection of Authority*. And not only authority as an abstract concept; these Americans are weak on *Religiosity, Traditional Family, Propriety,* and *National Pride*. But while they consider traditional authority passé, they are in constant pursuit of new authorities on the ideal lifestyle choices: the coolest and most politically correct coffee beans; Pinot Grigio or Cabernet Sauvignon; Alaska this year or Costa Rica—or both?

The rejection of authority here gives rise to two strains of values that dominate the profile of this region: the first revolves around flexibility, experimentation (both personal and social), and idealism, and the second revolves around rebellion, hedonism, and thrill-seeking.

The flexibility and idealism are plain to see. Pacific residents are the strongest in America on the trend *Adaptability to Complexity*, being comfortable with multiplicity and change in many areas of life. Nor do they depend on institutions to anchor their personal identities; strong on *Global Consciousness* and *Culture Sampling*, Pacific residents see themselves as citizens of a small world and derive pleasure and fulfillment from exploring cultures from around the globe, whether through travel or at a neighbour's home. Moreover, for these Americans, culture sampling need not be limited to the grade school food fair: residents of the ethnically diverse Pacific region are more likely than any other Americans to report that they'd be happy if someone in their family married someone of a different race and that children from mixed backgrounds enjoy a doubly rich heritage (the value *Racial Fusion*).

The flexibility and openness of West Coast dwellers also gives rise to a curiosity that verges on the spiritual. Strong on the trends *Mysterious Forces* and *Interest in the Unexplained,* they believe that inexplicable forces are at work in their lives, forces that intrigue and inspire them more than any other Americans. They're also the most likely to try to pay attention to *Intuition and Impulse* and to sometimes act on these extra-rational feelings. (Don't ask.)

In keeping with this region's reputation for youth worship (which may be the reason for its high score on *Equal Relationship with Youth*), Pacific dwellers are stronger than other Americans on the thrill-seeking trends *Penchant for Risk* and *Pursuit of Intensity.* Whether in real life or through entertainment, these Americans like to imagine themselves living fast and striving for intense experience. And in view of their rejection of conventional sexual mores (Pacific dwellers score low not just on *Traditional Family* but also on *Traditional Gender Identity*), it follows that these Americans score higher than any others on the trend *Sexual Permissiveness.*

As for the region's economic attitudes, faith in *Entrepreneurialism* is strong; these frontier individualists are attracted to making a living without a boss. It's no accident that the West Coast became a mecca for entrepreneurs, especially during the tech boom of the 1990s. Little sympathy is granted to those who don't achieve success, however: strong on *Just Deserts,* these Americans believe that people usually end up with the success or failure they deserve.

Pacific Values Profile

Strongest		Weakest	
Rejection of Authority	132	Traditional Family	79
Adaptability to Complexity	128	Religiosity	68
Global Consciousness	129	National Pride	71
Culture Sampling	140	Propriety	74
Racial Fusion	120	Traditional Gender Identity	68
Mysterious Forces	124		
Interest in the Unexplained	127		
Intuition and Impulse	118		
Equal Relationship with Youth	121		
Penchant for Risk	137		
Pursuit of Intensity	122		
Sexual Permissiveness	130		
Entrepreneurialism	121		
Just Deserts	120		

low (under 80)
neutral (80–120)
high (over 120)

PLAINS

A robust individualism, tempered by a traditional deference to authority, characterizes this region. Indeed, the Plains[8] might be described as the most quintessentially American of the nine regions in its values.

Among Plains dwellers we find a strong streak of traditionalism, manifested in *Religiosity,* a sense of *Propriety,* and a belief in *Obedience to Authority.* They also register a deep sense of *Everyday Ethics,* being matched only by those in the South Atlantic region in their willingness to tell a restaurant server they've been undercharged or to report to their bank that they've received a cheque in error.

But although they believe in old-fashioned respect and propriety, these Americans are unwilling to let their traditionalism interfere with their individualism. For example, they may believe in authority, but they reject the idea that it should accrue to people through arbitrary characteristics like gender: this segment rejects *Patriarchy* and is by far the strongest segment on *Gender Parity*. If a woman can do the job, let her do it well and attain the *American Dream* in which this segment believes so strongly.

Residents of the Plains have the highest score of all the regions on *Personal Control*. They strive to assert it in all areas of life, and use the services of professionals selectively (preferring to do things themselves). They also have great faith in those who exercise autonomy in the workplace; this is the strongest segment on the value *Confidence in Small Business*.

Americans living in the Plains states by and large reject the idea that they cannot change the course of their lives or the course of events in the world: they're weak on *Fatalism, Ecological Fatalism,* and *Anomie-Aimlessness.* Moreover, although they're too individualistic to be joiners (they're weak on *Community Involvement*), they reject the political fatalism inherent in *Civic Apathy*. In keeping with their belief that individuals have the right and the responsibility to control their own lives, these Americans have little interest in *Active Government.* But Plains dwellers don't go so far as to embrace the Darwinist trend *Just Deserts.* Nor do they believe that individual drive and desire trump all other ends; perhaps reined in by their *Religiosity,* they are weakest of all on *Acceptance of Violence.*

With their personal financial optimism, as manifested in their high scores on *Financial Security* and *American Dream,* this segment is sanguine about daily life in America. They're weak on the trend *Fear of Violence,* and report that they experience very little *Everyday Rage.*

They're also less interested than residents of other regions in the pursuits that, according to value change over time, increasingly pre-occupy many Americans: consumption and thrill-seeking. They're weaker than average on *Penchant for Risk* and *Attraction for Crowds* (a trend that also relates to this region's loner ethos), and register little desire to escape their daily lives into a fantasy or private bubble of experience *(Personal Escape)*. Moreover, Plains dwellers are among the weakest on numerous consumption-oriented trends, including *Importance of Brand, Buying on Impulse,* and *Confidence in Advertising*. These individualists are less likely than other Americans to seek to impress people with their possessions. They may strive after the *American Dream,* but for them financial success implies freedom and autonomy more than possessions.

Plains Values Profile

Strongest		Weakest	
Religiosity	127	Fatalism	64
Propriety	141	Ecological Fatalism	76
Obedience to Authority	132	Anomie-Aimlessness	52
Everyday Ethics	120	Community Involvement	76
Gender Parity	131	Civic Apathy	78
American Dream	118	Active Government	56
Personal Control	128	Just Deserts	71
Selective Use of Professional Services	125	Acceptance of Violence	68
Confidence in Small Business	126	Fear of Violence	74
Financial Security	119	Everyday Rage	53
		Penchant for Risk	70
		Attraction for Crowds	75
		Personal Escape	73
		Importance of Brand	71
		Buying on Impulse	80
		Confidence in Advertising	77

low (under 80)

neutral (80–120)

high (over 120)

SOUTH ATLANTIC

Compared with most of the other regions, South Atlantic[9] residents are, in a word, conservative. They have traditional values with regard to religion, the family, ethics, and the economy. The priorities that emerge from their values profile could not be much clearer.

Along with the Deep South and the Plains, this region is among the three most religious in the United States. South Atlantic dwellers are the most likely of all Americans to report that they're on an active personal *Spiritual Quest*. But making religion personal isn't the same as personalizing it, and this region is second only to the Deep South in its rejection of *Religion à la Carte*. Instead, religion and its demands are, for these Americans, non-negotiable. The strongly held value of *Obedience to Authority* dictates that they must not question or selectively heed the dictates of their religious leaders. And from religion flows a strict code of ethics by which they try to live.

South Atlantic dwellers believe in the family model they hear about at church: father-led, with two married parents of the opposite sex and their biological children. Residents here are among the three weakest (along with the Deep South and Texarkana) on the value *Flexible Families*. It's a truism for these Americans strong on *Patriarchy* that Father knows best and that his dominion extends over his wife and most certainly over his children (they're the weakest of all on *Equal Relationship with Youth*). And not only are they attached to a single model of the family but to their own particular families. This is the single strongest segment on *Primacy of the Family*, being the most likely to report that they put family ahead of all other priorities in life, and that their happiest moments are spent with their families.

Since strict gender roles underpin this region's ideal of family, it's not surprising that these Americans are especially strong in their rejection of *Flexible Gender Identity*. The idea of men and women dressing and behaving in ways not traditionally associated with their own gender also offends this segment's sense of *Propriety*.

This sense of *Propriety* is at the root of their *Concern for Appearance*. South Atlantic dwellers report that they take a great deal of care in choosing their clothes and constructing their personal appearance. It's so important to these Americans that it affects their sense of personal well-being; they're strong on the trend *Look Good Feel Good*. This emphasis on personal appearance can sometimes be underpinned by a desire to ostentatiously display wealth: expensive clothes and jewellery can help outer-directed people feel good by looking good (read, rich). South Atlantic residents, however, aren't notable consumers, since for them looking good means looking respectable—dressing appropriately for the occasion and in keeping with one's gender and station in life.

South Atlantic Values Profile

Strongest		Weakest	
Religiosity	123	Religion à la Carte	76
Spiritual Quest	127	Flexible Families	80
Obedience to Authority	118	Equal Relationship with Youth	80
Everyday Ethics	120	Flexible Gender Identity	83
Patriarchy	131		
Primacy of the Family	120		
Propriety	129		
Concern for Appearance	125		
Look Good Feel Good	122		
American Dream	119		
Work Ethic	125		
Time Stress	129		

◼ low (under 80)

▨ neutral (80–120)

▢ high (over 120)

Wealth is certainly not immaterial here: residents of the South Atlantic region aspire to and believe in the *American Dream*. But their traditional values (and perhaps their religious modesty) keep them from being too covetous; it's not just the trappings of wealth to which these Americans aspire but a global version of success, moral as well as material, that they hope to achieve through their strong *Work Ethic*.

And so between working toward the American Dream, spending time with family, cultivating a meticulous personal appearance, and devoting time to religious practice, South Atlantic dwellers are feeling the greatest *Time Stress* of any American region.

TEXARKANA

Three dominant strains of values stand out in the profile of the Texarkana[10] region: tradition, status, and hostility.

Among the traditional values of this region are *Patriarchy, Propriety,* and *Traditional Gender Identity*. These trends reinforce one another, since domestic and social order depend on the authority of the ruling patriarch. In order for a gender-based system of social organization to hold, *Traditional Gender Identity* must be observed: men must be men and women, women. *Propriety* in this context implies not only modesty but adherence to rules of gender-coded dress and behaviour. For a woman to dress and behave in a masculine way undermines male authority; for a man to dress and behave in a feminine way violates the male responsibility to protect and lead the home. And so this region's rejection of *Flexible Families* speaks both to its belief in the importance of a family model that enshrines patriarchal authority (which single-parent and same-sex households cannot) and to its belief in a gendered division of labour that relies on fixed gender identities.

Residents of the Texarkana region are strong on several trends associated with aspiration and status. They believe deeply in the *American Dream*—that they or someone in their family could "make it" on a grand scale by becoming president, for example, or by achieving great wealth or celebrity. (Those who've made it command respect, not suspicion, from Texarkana residents: this region has the second highest score on *Confidence in Big Business*.) And since they harbour a strong belief that the United States remains a true meritocracy, it follows that these Americans register a deep *Need for Status Recognition*. In this world view, status flows from success, which in turn flows from personal virtues such as intelligence and industriousness; Texarkana residents want their status to be understood as signifying not just wealth but the quality of their character.

Because status holds deep meaning for this segment, they feel a connection between their personal appearance and their sense of well-being *(Look Good Feel Good)*. Texarkana residents are also more likely than the average American to report an interest in *Ostentatious Consumption*—the purchase and display of possessions that demonstrate their success in pursuing the American Dream. *Dallas,* the 1980s prime-time soap opera, was an early document of the ostentation that tends to bubble up from the ground along with this region's black gold. Remaining abreast of all that their possessions signify, these Americans pay attention to advertising and are often happy to let it coax them to consume.

Although much of this region's profile suggests a stereotypical American world view—energetic material striving contained in a traditional moral framework—it also exhibits a strain of disengagement and hostility. Texarkana is the single strongest region on the trend *Everyday Rage,* suggesting that its residents are not entirely pleased with the state of their society and are willing to express their frustrations in their daily encounters with others. (Don't mess with Texas.) For many, this dissatisfaction extends into fear; Texarkana dwellers are strong on the trend *Fear of Violence.*

The region is also among the strongest on the trend *Xenophobia,* suggesting that these Americans may attribute some of the deterioration they believe is occurring in American society to outsiders arriving from other countries.

Nevertheless, they're less likely than other Americans to try to change what they see as society's flaws through political action: this is the single weakest region on the trend *Civic Engagement.* Also weak on the value *More Power for Politics,* these Americans show little interest in channelling their *Everyday Rage* into organized civic initiatives.

Texarkana Values Profile

Strongest		Weakest	
Patriarchy	138	Flexible Families	80
Propriety	141	Civic Engagement	84
Traditional Gender Identity	141	More Power for Politics	71
American Dream	125		
Confidence in Big Business	128		
Need for Status Recognition	122		
Look Good Feel Good	139		
Ostentatious Consumption	122		
Advertising as Stimulus	125		
Everyday Rage	143		
Fear of Violence	123		

■ low (under 80)

■ neutral (80–120)

□ high (over 120)

L IKE OTHER LARGE COUNTRIES such as Canada, India, and Brazil, America contains considerable diversity, both ecological and cultural. This diversity is fostered not only by the country's size and physical properties but also, of course, by its historical relations with its neighbours and its traditions of immigration and internal migration. When the phenomenon known as globalization was first widely discussed, some worried that it would lead to the erosion of local cultures around the world. And in many cases the loss of local culture was code for one thing: "Americanization." But even as many around the world feared the trampling of their local particularities by the march of Hollywood movies and the usual U.S. brands, some Americans were fretting over the loss of their own local quirks. Identical big-box stores sprang up in every corner of the nation; neighbourhood cafés were bowled over by Starbucks, selling option-overload; main streets were blown away by price-slashing Wal-Marts; shopping malls contained all the same chains, which contained all the same merchandise, which was flogged with the same signage and slogans on the same days. The official Gap mixtape rang out from Seattle to New York to Miami to Tucson.

Today, the hoopla around globalization has abated. Its component phenomena—changes in media, trade relations, and transportation—have proceeded at varying rates with consequences intended and otherwise. And, as it turns out, local culture remains—both in America's many distinct corners and around the world. In 1984 the Canadian literary critic Northrop Frye remarked on some of his compatriots' anxiety about the Americanization of their own country thus: "What people mean when they speak of Americanization has been just as lethal to American culture as it has been to Canadian culture. It's a kind of levelling down which I think every concerned citizen of democracy should fight, whether he is a Canadian or an American." The values profiles I have just described suggest that America's regions have, if we accept the definition of Americanization as homogenization, resisted their own Americanization by remaining distinct not only in their topography but in their values.

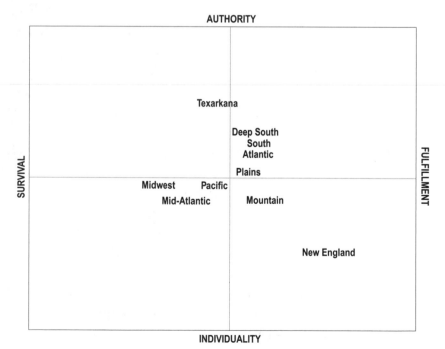

Combined Data, 1992, 1996, 2000, 2004

five

The Great Backlash

There is one expanding horror in American life. It is that our long odyssey
toward liberty, democracy, and freedom-for-all may be achieved in such a way
that utopia remains forever closed, and we live in freedom and hell ...
—Norman Mailer

T HE YEAR 2003 was not an easy one for potatoes in the United States.
It was bad enough that they were so violently scorned by a suddenly carb-
phobic nation in the grip of diets that saw the starchy spud as the enemy
of pert buttocks and firm tummies everywhere. But things got worse. The
potato found itself dragged into a limp political drama when, in protest
against French opposition to the war in Iraq, some members of Congress
called upon Americans to begin referring to salty, deep-fried potato spears
as Freedom Fries. The new name for one of America's least healthful foods
was adopted by some and derided by others. The French embassy had no
response other than to note that French fries came from Belgium. (One of
the co-authors of the original statement on Freedom Fries from the House
of Representatives, Walter Jones [R.– N.C.], later regretted his pro-war
stance and said of the fry campaign, "I wish it had never happened."[1]

I suspect that those who scoffed at the name Freedom Fries (not to
mention the fries' poor cousin, Freedom Toast—toast also had a tough
year) and those who thought the name change was an excellent idea had
more or less the same reason: it was just so ostentatiously, unapologetically
American.

"Freedom" is trotted out to serve endless purposes—political, rhetorical, and emotional—when Americans discuss the ideals toward which
their nation should strive. And when organizations as loathsome to each
other as the National Rifle Association and the American Civil Liberties
Union cite the same word as their raison d'être, you know you've got a
semantic precision problem on your hands.

How the ideal of freedom should be made manifest in American life
has been one of that society's enduring preoccupations. Traditionally,
Americans have managed to balance the very minimum in state inter-
vention with powerful (at some times suffocating) social codes of
morality and propriety. It may sound alarmist when American moralists
fret about divorce or same-sex marriage or rap music or pink hair
"unravelling the very fabric of society" (an oft-repeated phrase). But
this is a society where religion and strictly enforced social mores have
long served to counterbalance the uniquely vast quantity of freedom
individuals enjoy. It is not altogether unreasonable, therefore, to project
that a diminished adherence to a shared, strict idea of morality (and of
the fiery consequences of transgressing that morality) might indeed be
a more serious problem in America than it would be in Denmark or
France or even Canada.

One of the hallmarks of progressivism, in America as elsewhere, is a
sense that individuals can construct meaningful moral and spiritual
codes for themselves, or at least explore a number of faith traditions
and philosophical ideas before adhering to one or another, and that
people should respect one another's choices in this regard. Good advice
can come from many sources: find some that makes sense to you, and
follow it.

This idea of a flexible, syncretic approach to being good has become so
pervasive in industrialized nations that in an appearance before a group of
Catholic youth in Cologne, Germany, in August 2005, Pope Benedict
XVI saw fit to call it by name. He cautioned his young flock against the
dangers of "do-it-yourself religion," warning that spirituality isn't like
shopping; you can't pick and choose. There is one true path and you're
either on it or you're astray. In this paradigm of clear right and wrong,

respect for what you don't agree with isn't doing anyone any favours. Or, in the words of a T-shirt on one delegate to the 2004 Republican convention, "Intolerance is a beautiful thing."

In the first two chapters of this book I described the movement of American society into the lower-left quadrant of our map—toward values of brash individualism and hard hedonism. I also explained that politically engaged Americans, those who reported that they were certain to vote in the next election, were on a different trajectory. They were moving back up the map, embracing anew the more traditional values of their parents and grandparents: religion, duty, patriotism.

America is a fascinating case in this respect. Canada and Western Europe have generally been, as long as their values have been measured, evolving down and right on the map, toward ever greater flexibility, openness to diversity, and emphasis on personal fulfillment. Americans, on the other hand, are on average steering clear of the postmodern values in the lower-right quadrant. This is fine with ardent conservatives, for whom the only livable space on the map is at the top, where *Traditional Family, National Pride,* and *Obedience to Authority* reside. But to progressives, their compatriots' unwillingness to join them in the lower-right quadrant means that, recalling Norman Mailer's epigraph, the door to utopia remains closed.

Americans, or at least a vocal segment of the youth population, had a flirtation with the utopia on offer in the lower-right quadrant during what has come to be called America's cultural revolution. But deep social change didn't follow those idealistic young people down to Max Yasgur's farm in Woodstock, New York, for a muddy baptism into a world of free love, unbleached cotton, and organic produce. Instead, some Americans headed back up the map to join Reverend James Dobson, where they would dare to discipline themselves and each other. The rest headed into the lower-left quadrant to see, like hip-hop superstar 50 Cent, whether they would get rich or die trying. In this chapter, I will describe the unfolding of these journeys as I see them, situating our data in the context of some key events in America over the course of the last century.

THREE GREAT AND INTERRELATED "ISMS"—socialism, idealism, and hedonism—transformed America in the middle of the twentieth century and generated a reaction that has coalesced into the now-prevailing conservative movement in American politics. The forces of the new conservatism—grassroots religious movements, idea-generating think tanks and magazines, and smart political and fundraising machinery— began to gather in the early 1960s, with the goal of challenging the centrist-progressive consensus that dominated America. Conservatives have succeeded in fracturing that consensus in the political sphere, but the cultural sphere, as we saw in Chapter 1, continues to a great extent to travel down a version of the path that so alarmed conservatives in the 1960s and 1970s.

The new conservatism, which came to dominate a Republican Party that had for decades seemed to more or less go along with the progressive consensus,[2] was helped to power by the perception among the American public that the Democratic Party had drifted too far to the left to address the concerns of ordinary citizens, especially on social issues. A popular slogan of the 1980 Reagan presidential campaign was "You didn't leave the Democratic Party; the Democratic Party left you." When it pledged to address the frustration of Americans in the 1970s, many of whom had previously considered themselves liberals and/or Democrats, this new conservatism, under the preternaturally likeable Ronald Reagan, finally gained its foothold in the mainstream. Thereafter, two events accelerated the evolution of the current conservative movement from a fringe reaction to America's dominant ideology: the collapse of communism in 1989 and the rise of terrorism, made devastatingly apparent on September 11, 2001.

But in order to understand this conservative backlash, we must look more closely at the three great isms in order of their appearance.

SOCIALISM

Whereas socialism was introduced into European societies by political parties that represented the proletarian workers, it came to America as a reluctant reaction to the devastation wrought by the Great Depression.

In 1932 unemployment in the United States had risen to 23.6 percent. Since the crash of 1929 over 13 million people had lost their jobs and the GNP had fallen by 31 percent. Americans were dissatisfied with Herbert Hoover's response to the economic catastrophe, which they saw as too little too late. In his Democratic nomination speech, Franklin Roosevelt outlined his own proposed response to the unprecedented financial strife gripping the nation and declared, "I pledge you, I pledge myself, to a new deal for the American people." Desperate citizens were ready to turn from their traditional reliance on market forces (unalloyed by much government control) and toward the state activism of this New Deal. Roosevelt's promise of relief, recovery, and reform was a beacon.

Even after World War II drastically improved economic circumstances in America, the state activism that began with the New Deal was evident in the 1944 GI Bill, continued through the 1950s with the construction of the Interstate Highway System, and accelerated in the 1960s with Lyndon Johnson's Great Society and War on Poverty. Even Dwight Eisenhower, the only Republican president to be elected in the years spanning the New Deal and the Great Society, was not substantially more hostile to government involvement in the economy than his Democratic predecessors and successors. Indeed, Eisenhower might be surprised at his Republican confreres' efforts to privatize Social Security in the first decade of the twenty-first century, having written in 1956 that any party that attempted such a thing would be banished to the dustbin of American political history.[3]

The Johnson administration, with its racial equality measures and its War on Poverty, is often considered the high-water mark of America's flirtation with the social welfare state. But Richard Nixon introduced no radical reversal when it came to social spending. Nixon won the 1969 election by appealing to what he called the "silent majority": that segment of the American public dismayed by the general drift of the Democratic Party on social issues (racial equality measures, anti-war demonstrations, sharply rising crime rates, and the excesses of the 1960s counterculture). But while Nixon promised a more conservative approach to social issues, his administration's spending habits reflected no particular affinity with conservative fiscal priorities. In fact, both federal spending and federal regulation grew more quickly under Nixon than they had under Johnson.[4] The Nixon administration increased Social Security payments by 20 percent and introduced affirmative action, the Environmental Protection Agency, the National Oceanic and Atmospheric Administration, the Drug Enforcement Administration, the Cost of Living Council, and the Occupational Safety and Health Administration.

The Ford administration—which proceeded gingerly in the wake of the Watergate scandal—and the Carter administration continued in much the same vein. Only in 1980 did the tide turn in earnest. Ronald Reagan, who had once been an FDR Democrat, declared that government was the problem and not the solution. It was morning again in America, he announced, inviting his fellow citizens to awaken from the nightmare of socialism and behold once more the American Dream in its purity. Thus did the new conservative agenda begin dismantling the version of socialism that had become established public policy in America.

"Sidney bought that jacket when it was morning in America."

IDEALISM

The middle of the twentieth century also saw the evolution of a new progressive idealism in America. Its first major expression was the civil rights movement, whose roots are commonly traced to Brown v. Board of Education, the 1954 Supreme Court decision that eliminated the legal basis of school segregation. But while Brown was an important affirmation of the struggle to end the "separate but equal" doctrine that had consigned black children to their own often grossly underfunded schools since the Civil War, it may have been a greater watershed for opponents of civil rights than for its advocates. Michael J. Klarman argues in his book *From Jim Crow to Civil Rights* that the shift in American attitudes about race can more credibly be traced to World War II, a war against racist fascists in which black soldiers fought for their country in a segregated army. (Harry Truman desegregated the U.S. army in 1948, perhaps taking his cue from the Brooklyn Dodgers, who had signed Jackie Robinson the previous year.)

Black veterans came home to a country for which they had been prepared to die and in which they were no longer willing to accept their status as second-class citizens. A movement began to take shape, and white Americans, in some quarters, were increasingly sympathetic. Black activists were supported in their quest for equality by idealists (many from the North) who joined them in freedom marches throughout the South. The culmination of the movement was Lyndon Johnson's 1964 Civil Rights Act. The Voting Rights Act of 1965 followed, and by 1973 it had increased the number of black elected officials in eleven southern states by a factor of ten.[5]

When the Nixon administration introduced affirmative action in 1969, some saw it as an attempt to drive a wedge between white and black workers, and so for a time idealism clashed with socialism. Clarence Mitchell, then director of the National Association for the Advancement of Colored People (NAACP), attacked quotas as a "calculated attempt coming right from the president's desk to break up the coalition between Negroes and labor unions. Most of the social progress in this country has resulted from this alliance."[6]

Intentionally or no, these activist programs did generate opposition from some working-class whites. The more prominent push-back against racial equality measures came from southern racists, whose most infamous leader was former Alabama governor and two-time presidential candidate George Wallace. But northern cities to which southern blacks had migrated after the war experienced their own strife around both labour issues and school busing. Even some Northerners who had called for the desegregation of southern schools were surprised at the difficulty of fully integrating their own children's schools. (Boston, that bastion of progressivism, underwent famous unrest as it introduced busing for "racial balance" in the mid '70s.)

In addition to civil rights, several other movements characterized mid-century idealism in America; two of these, environmentalism and feminism, are intimately related. Rachel Carson's *Silent Spring,* published in 1962, was the *Communist Manifesto* of the environmental movement: Carson's book was the first, and still most famous, wake-up call that we were destroying the planet that sustained human existence and that had fostered organic life since it began. Environmentalists, like the civil rights advocates, had their victories. Perhaps the most significant was the 1970 Clean Air Act (an overhaul of 1963 legislation) that set National Ambient Air Quality Standards, imposed limits on emissions from automobiles and new industrial pollution sources, and gave citizens the right to take legal action against any party—including the government—violating these standards.

At the same time, American women were launching the second wave of the feminist movement, the first having propelled the American suffragette movement and having resulted in American women being granted the vote in 1921. In 1963 Betty Friedan published *The Feminine Mystique,* a book based in part on a survey she conducted among the women in her 1942 graduating class at Smith College. The book sold a million copies and galvanized a generation of middle-class American women by speaking about "the problem that has no name": the nagging dissatisfaction of middle-class American housewives who felt that their lives, activities, and worth were being defined by their husbands and children.

In 1971 Gloria Steinem and others founded *Ms.* magazine, which, despite being described by one male columnist as "C-sharp on an un-tuned piano," a note "of petulance, of bitchiness, or nervous fingernails screeching across a blackboard," sold out its one-shot test run of 300,000 copies in eight days and immediately became a regular publication with a substantial list of subscribers.

As discussion opened up among American women about their experiences and political goals, and as the voices in the conversation became more diverse, the feminist movement gained steam. Much of the formal political branch of the feminist movement coalesced around an effort to enshrine gender equality in the American constitution with the Equal Rights Amendment. The ERA enjoyed support at the federal level, being passed by the House of Representatives in 1971 and the Senate in 1972, and gained President Nixon's endorsement. But it never gained the kind of state support necessary for a constitutional amendment, and effectively died on the table in 1982.

HEDONISM

Socialism and idealism defined the American polity for four decades, but the 1960s were more, much more, than the lofty idealism of the civil rights movement and the government activism of the Great Society. It was also the decade of a new hedonism, better known as the sexual revolution, and it was this hedonism that most profoundly transformed American culture and everyday life. Veterans of the revolution used to say "If you remember the sixties, you weren't there," meaning of course that if you weren't lost in a fog of sex, drugs, and rock 'n' roll, you never really experienced the decade in its quintessential psychedelic form.

The moms and dads who formed families in record numbers after World War II felt deeply that through hard work and discipline they could realize the American Dream. The New Deal and the war had put capitalism back on its feet, and now a new generation could enjoy the entitlements of the post-Depression, post-war Affluent Society. A generation of baby boomers were encouraged to think for themselves by parents who wished for their children all the life, liberty, and happiness that their own youth had denied them.

The first entitlement of the new affluence was a suburban house. Owning one's own home, today perhaps the most fundamental promise of the American Dream, was until the middle of the twentieth century possible for only a minority of Americans. In 1934, when the Federal Housing Administration was established, just four in ten American households owned the places where they lived.[7] Following World War II, however, the Federal Housing Administration (FHA) and Veterans' Administration loan programs provided mortgages for over eleven million new houses. This assistance, combined with post-war economic growth, meant that people of the middle class increasingly expected to own their homes.[8]

These houses were for the most part located in newly built, low-density suburbs on meandering crescents away from distant downtown work-places and newly constructed shopping malls. In 1950 just 23 percent of Americans lived in the suburbs. That number had risen to over 30 percent by 1960 and to over 40 percent by 1980, and today the majority of Americans call the suburbs home.[9] Both economic and social factors contributed to the initial dispersal of the population away from urban areas. The post-war period saw tremendous government support for state and local roadways, not to mention the Interstate Highway Act of 1956. And many FHA mortgages on brand-new suburban houses were cheaper than paying rent in a downtown apartment.

Americans were also attracted to suburban neighbourhoods with people whose ethnicities and incomes were like their own. The suburbs as a category were diverse (the so-called white flight from racially diverse urban centres was only a small part of the story of American suburbanization; Americans of many races fled the cities in favour of perceived safety and peace and quiet), but individual neighbourhoods did tend to be fairly homogeneous. They still do.

Densities in the new suburbs were too low to support the kind of public transit made possible by the grid systems that characterized the higher density of urban centres. And different areas of life—work, home, leisure, civic activities, schools—were now spread out across much greater distances. The mastermind of the earliest versions of the enclosed shopping mall, Victor Gruen, worried that suburban Americans in the 1950s and '60s were living "detached lives in detached homes."[10] The automobile became a lifeline.

And the family car wasn't only essential for getting around; it was a symbol of one's position in the status hierarchy of the great American middle class. For the American status seeker, the automobile evolved from the utilitarian horseless carriage to the pre-eminent symbol of success— one that required renewal every two or three years as Detroit churned out ever more ostentatious expressions of the American lust for mobility. The car was embedded in the American psyche; a virtual clash of symbols could be heard when General Motors immortalized Marilyn Monroe's ample breasts on the grille of their 1957 Cadillac, inspiring Elvis Presley to acquire a multicoloured fleet. Cars were to middle-class Americans of the 1950s and early '60s what a European bride or a chateau-inspired mansion had been to the nouveaux riches in the Gilded Age of the late nineteenth century.

The hedonism of the 1950s was both material and experiential, but in each case it was "soft." Well-appointed suburban homes and the latest American-model car defined the material; a well-deserved martini (or two) at 6:00 p.m. was Dad's reward for a hard day's work before he sat down with Mom and the kids to a home-cooked dinner. That soft hedonism was soon to give way, however, to the harder hedonism of the rebellious 1960s, when sex, drugs, and rock 'n' roll emerged as a brazen cultural triad.

The populous generation of baby boomers were brought up by mothers (and, after 6:00, fathers who knew best) who dared replace the homespun wisdom of their own mothers and fathers with the "scientific" counsel of pediatrician Dr. Benjamin Spock. His 1946 owner's manual for parents, *The Common Sense Book of Baby and Child Care*, had as its central message "Trust yourself." Parents were advised to abandon the rigid rules of experts (even of their own mothers and fathers) who cautioned too often against spoiling children and instead "to respect children because they're human beings and they deserve respect, and they'll grow up to be better people."

Not everyone was impressed by this egalitarian, we're-all-human-beings approach. Spock drew criticism from the Reverend Norman Vincent Peale (author of 1952's famous book *The Power of Positive Thinking*) as well as Vice-President Spiro Agnew, who found him too permissive. But critics could not rein in Spock's runaway success. His book went on to sell 50 million copies in thirty languages and would help transform the traditional "strict father" parenting model to the "nurturing parent" of the '50s and '60s.

These well-nurtured boomers experienced an energized adolescence, exchanging the waltz and foxtrot for the spontaneous (and often lascivious) moves inspired first by Elvis (the Pelvis) Presley, then the Beatles, and then the Rolling Stones. As dance-floor gyrations gave way to horizontal versions, excited boomers were drawn to practise the free love that the intrepid Dr. Alfred Kinsey had brought out of the closet a decade before. Word began to get out: masturbation wouldn't make you blind, oral sex wouldn't make you sterile, and sex in general didn't necessarily set you on the greased chute to damnation. (And anyway, maybe no one was watching: *Time* magazine caught up with Nietzsche in 1966, wondering on its April 8 cover, "Is God Dead?")

Along with attitudinal changes toward sex came the small practical matter of the birth control pill. In 1957 the FDA approved a drug called Enovid that was intended to treat severe menstrual disorders. The FDA ordered that the drug carry a label warning users that it prevented ovulation. The American public took the warning to heart: by 1959, half a million women seemed to have developed "severe menstrual disorders" that necessitated the prescription of Enovid. By 1973 ten million American women were on the Pill (now explicitly used for birth control, which had been illegal in some states when Enovid was first approved), including nearly a third of Catholic women, despite the Church's proscriptions. As the automobile had propelled their parents to new heights of mobility, so the Pill propelled boomer kids to new heights of orgiastic ecstasy. A society that had dared not speak the word became obsessed with sex; and for youth, that meant sex before marriage without consequences: heaven on earth.

Added to this explosion of erotic energy were the drugs both soft (marijuana) and hard (LSD) that quickly migrated from the nation's fringes to its colleges and universities. To many, the change seemed incredibly rapid: LSD was virtually unknown in the early '60s; most Americans were so ignorant of its applications that it remained legal until 1966. It was a party not seen since the Roaring Twenties, but this time the roaring was suffused with a lot more political meaning. And this time the hangover wouldn't be an economic catastrophe but rather a conservative backlash by tens of millions of Americans who did not like the noise of this party and, in the echoing words of the 1975 film *Network,* were mad as hell and not going to take it any more.

THE ANGRY ISM: THE NEW CONSERVATISM

The hedonism of the '60s rocked many—but shocked more. If the social change that exploded in that decade was unprecedented, so was the backlash it generated. The recharged American conservative movement announced itself politically in 1964 with Barry Goldwater; gained power, esteem, and mainstream credibility with Ronald Reagan; and now with the re-election of George W. Bush has shown itself to be the establishment ideology of our time.

Conservatives of the past few decades are sometimes said to have been New Deal liberal democrats who, like Ronald Reagan, were "mugged by reality" in the 1960s and 70s. From the conservative perspective, these Americans were mugged by the big-government nanny-state policies that started with FDR's New Deal and culminated with Lyndon Johnson's Great Society. They were mugged by the court-ordered busing that threatened to integrate their children into predominantly black schools or, more likely, black kids into their white suburban enclaves—which to many Americans at the time seemed to threaten their children's education and thus their ticket to the American Dream. They were mugged by the extremism of the Black Panthers and the torching of great American cities in the riots of the late 1960s. They were mugged by the assassinations of a popular president, of a revered civil rights leader, and of a promising presidential candidate. They were mugged by an administration that got them into a foreign war that their country was losing and that ultimately killed over 50,000 of its sons. They were mugged (sometimes literally) by a crime wave. They were mugged by the excesses of hedonism and the militants of the anti-war/anti-draft and free speech movements inspired by bearded neo-Marxist professors like Herbert Marcuse. America's youth seemed to be going mad, and its system of higher education seemed to be helping them.

And if the '60s hadn't provided enough evidence, the '70s were proof positive that America was veering seriously off track. Watergate and the peace without honour in Vietnam were serious blows to two of America's most revered institutions: its presidency and its military. The '70s saw the first forced resignation of an American president and the nation's first military defeat since the British burned the White House in 1813. Added to this was the stagflation that finally put the brakes on an economy that had seemed to be on automatic pilot since the end of World War II. The 1973–74 and 1979–80 oil price shocks, inflicted on unsuspecting Americans by OPEC, made the price of gas skyrocket and led to shortages that created mile-long lines at the nation's gas stations. Speed limits on interstate highways were lowered to 55 mph in a country that had come to both depend on and worship its cars and the freedom they symbolized. The economy stopped growing, unemployment and prices rose, and the so-called misery index of the combined unemployment and inflation rates hit double digits by the end of the decade. The numbers were all wrong and the symbols were worse as Democratic president Jimmy Carter sought re-election. And as if trouble on the home front wasn't enough, the embattled president who had famously admitted to a "crisis of the spirit" in the nation found himself incapable of freeing Americans held hostage in far-off Iran.

Beginning with William F. Buckley in the 1950s and undaunted by the failed candidacy of Barry Goldwater in 1964, with intellectual input from the likes of Milton Friedman, Norman Podhoretz, Irving Kristol, Daniel Patrick Moynihan, and others, and financed by a few very wealthy families, the American right began to create think tanks to generate ideas in opposition to what they saw as the excesses of the socialism, idealism, and hedonism that had reached their zenith in the 1960s. As time went on, these new conservatives began to find allies among the Christian right, then known as the Moral Majority. The intellectuals hated big government and what they considered the out-of-control idealism of affirmative action, busing, feminism, and environmentalism. The Moral Majority hated the over-the-top hedonism. The family that hates together stays together, and this family stuck together to get conservative politics back in the game in the United States. Their success was huge.

The movement gained coherence, discipline, and strength for four decades. It now controls the Republican Party and exerts considerable influence in the Democratic Party, too—both by framing political discourse and by continuing to actively attract and support smart, articulate spokespeople. (Ask a Democrat whether he or she is a liberal and witness the shocked horror and vigorous denials; it's no accident that "liberal" has become a dirty word in American politics.) The new conservative movement has a significant majority in the House of Representatives and a slight majority in the Senate. It controls the executive branch and, if the Bush White House has its way, will occupy five of nine seats on the Supreme Court by the time Dubya packs up his desk in 2008. FDR could only dream of such ascendance.

The most extreme of these conservatives, at least from the perspective of America's embattled liberal progressives, wish to roll back the advances of socialism and transform American idealism from that of progressive boomers to the "traditional" ideals of Christianity, the father-led nuclear family, and competition for the American Dream in an ever freer market. They wish to continue the work begun in 1976 when the Supreme Court ruled there was nothing in the Constitution that precluded the states from invoking the death penalty, as thirty-eight of them do. They wish to continue the work of Howard Jarvis, who in 1978 persuaded his fellow Californians to adopt the anti-tax Proposition 13. (Profligate government spending under George Bush *fils*—mainly on the military and homeland security but also on a huge Medicare expansion, among other things— may become an increasingly thorny issue for the conservative family.) They wish to continue the work of the National Rifle Association, which interprets the second amendment's "well-regulated militias" as meaning that every American has the right to pack a .357 Magnum (and, in Texas, anti-tank weaponry) in self-defence. They wish to keep the words "under God," added to the Pledge of Allegiance in 1954 as a measure in the fight against godless communism, exactly where they are—and if the line between church and state gets blurry, all the better. They wish to complete the work of Phyllis Schlafly, who led the movement that killed the Equal Rights Amendment in 1982, as well as that of David Stockman, Ronald Reagan's economic guru, and push the country so far into debt that it will force Congress to further cut back "superfluous" social programs, leaving only enough tax money for the military, prisons, the police, and homeland security. They wish to complete the work of those who opposed Hillary Clinton's ill-fated socialist universal health care scheme, leaving Americans to shop among HMOs and pay whatever the insurance and pharmaceutical companies deem appropriate. They wish to build on Bill Clinton's 1996 reform of "welfare as we know it" by triaging the poor into those who will be inspired to replace welfare with one, two, or three jobs, those who will struggle by with handouts from relatives and the Salvation Army, and those who will just plain disappear to God knows where.

Socialism, idealism, and hedonism at home generated this Newtonian equal and opposite reaction of revived conservatism (of which the above is only one fanciful portrait). But events on the world stage have also played their part: the implosion of communism in Eastern Europe in 1989 turned America from first among equals, which it had been since World War II, into just plain first. The world's lone superpower is now able to go its own way in rejecting the International Criminal Court, Kyoto, and the land-mines treaty and ignoring the North American Free Trade Agreement and World Trade Organization rules it helped create and implored others to ratify.

America has always been wary of internationalism. Consistent with its traditional emphasis on individualism at home, on the world stage America has jealously guarded its own sovereignty against constraints imposed by the international community. But in its more recent position as the biggest, toughest kid on the block, America has altered its traditional posture toward the rest of the world beyond mere aloofness to assume a do-as-I-say-not-as-I-do dimension. This dimension is, of course, compounded by the Bush administration's "with us or against us" doctrine.

After the horror of 9/11, American unilateralism in the first, inchoate steps in the war on terror met with near universal domestic approval. It also enjoyed fairly broad support internationally, as America sought to destroy terrorist networks in Afghanistan and unseat the Taliban regime that had fostered them. As the war marched on toward new and sometimes shifting goals, some countries, most notably Great Britain, were willing to tag along on the course America dictated. But George W. Bush signalled decisively that as far as he was concerned the era of lasting allegiances and mutual back-scratching between nations was over. At the Gleneagles G-8 Summit, asked whether he would be more favourable toward Tony Blair's campaigns on African poverty and the environment because of Blair's loyalty to the United States in the war in Iraq, Bush replied, "I really don't view our relationship as one of quid pro quo. Tony Blair made decisions on what he thought was best for keeping the peace and winning the war on terror, as I did."[11] At the beginning of the twenty-first century, America does not have friends; it has assistants on short-term contract. As Defense Secretary Donald Rumsfeld remarked, "The mission determines the coalition."[12] Before 9/11, America was a lone superpower increasingly controlled by those who constituted the conservative reaction against the three isms. After 9/11, the hawkish neoconservatives, previously lurking in the wings of the conservative movement and flexing more muscle with word processors than with F-16s, have turned their gaze on the world. The politics of American conservative reaction, which have so drastically transformed their own nation since 1980, may now transform the world as America's leaders attempt to export their unique brand of freedom around the globe.

six

Reaching Beyond the Choir

There may be a lot of bad Republicans. There are no good Democrats.
—Ann Coulter, conservative pundit

*Dean … clarified his comment a day later to say that he was referring
to the Republican leadership, not to ordinary Republicans.*
—*The Washington Post,* reporting on Democratic National Committee
chair Howard Dean's qualification of his comment that "a lot of
[Republicans] have never made an honest living in their lives"

One of us! One of us!
—1932 horror film *Freaks*

I T'S RARE that any politician, no matter how rabidly partisan, no
matter how ideologically zealous, dumps explicitly on voters who
support the opposing party. It's something of a no-brainer that one
shouldn't insult the intelligence or judgment of those whose votes one
hopes to attract. But in a 50–50 nation where rhetoric is heated, it is a
trickier dance than it might seem: how does one insult the opposing
party, its leaders, and its principles while retaining a statesmanlike
dignity and flattering those who are still thinking about supporting the
enemy's obviously misguided policies and representatives?

Screaming heads like Ann Coulter, quoted above, hurl insults at
ordinary Americans all the time; the more outrageous, the greater the

book sales. (Not to mention Coulter's rumoured $25,000 fee for a speaking engagement, which brings to mind the Monty Python sketch in which a man walks into a room hoping to pay someone to argue intelligently with him but instead inadvertently enters the office of a purveyor of verbal abuse.) Perhaps most famously, Coulter has expressed longing for a terrorist attack at the offices of *The New York Times*. But when someone who actually *officially* represents a party, insults supporters of the other party, reprimand from both sides tends to be swift.

Politicians criticize their opponents, of course, and the opposing party's leadership. But usually the closest politicians get to insulting their opponents' *supporters* is suggesting that they've been deceived: these nice folks think they're voting for good people and good principles, but unfortunately they've been hoodwinked.

The disaster of condescending to voters by telling them that the candidate they're considering is *obviously* the wrong choice was made very clear in the 2004 presidential campaign when readers of Britain's *Guardian* newspaper wrote letters to an Ohio swing county informing them of what a bad idea it would be to re-elect George W. Bush. Not only did many very irritated Ohioans respond angrily on the *Guardian* website (one of the milder replies: "Real Americans aren't interested in your pansy-ass, tea-sipping opinions. If you want to save the world, begin with your own worthless corner of it"), but the county ultimately went red—not just in the face, but electorally as well. It's difficult to know whether the letter-writing campaign pushed anyone over the edge, but it's plausible to think that more than one swing voter, reflecting on this friendly advice from his new best friend and war-on-terror ally across the pond, shared the thoughts of a betrayed first-grader in the film *Rushmore*. "With friends like you, who needs friends?"

All this speaks to the difficulty true believers on both ends of the ideological spectrum face when they must convince voters in the middle to come to their side, without being seen as too smug or vitriolic and without letting their criticism of their opponents ever come across as disdain for those who are still considering electing them.

Because of this difficulty, much campaign rhetoric is about convincing people that they *already* share your goals and values, that they're *already* natural members of your party but just may not have realized it yet. You believe in hard work and ordinary Americans? You believe in families and safe communities? You believe in fairness and you want the best for your children? You're *already* a Republican. Or a Democrat. Promoting the idea that voters are already "one of us" leads to some very banal definitions of "us," but it handily sidesteps the problem of having to convince people of specific ideas with which they may disagree. A famous distortion of a statement made by former Canadian Prime Minister Kim Campbell is, however perverse, rather true: "An election campaign is no time to discuss serious issues."

In their efforts not to offend or alienate any potential supporter, politicians strive for vagueness that somehow manages to appear serious, resolute, and likeable. But at some point, in order to attract moderates, the core (politicians and their fervent supporters) must identify real common ground—if only a sliver of it. They have to iden-tify something—whether "values" or actual policy positions—on which the base and a good chunk of swing voters can agree, and then speak to that area of agreement, cementing the union between the choir and the less devout.

Values are a crucial part of political messaging, and have become a focal point in recent campaigns. This is not just because moralism has become an increasingly powerful force in American politics, giving rise to buzz phrases like "family values" and "moral values." It also has to do with a shift in the way people's personal identities are constructed, now that they're no longer so heavily dictated by their position in some production hierarchy (owner, manager, salesman, worker) or by demographic traits. Today, people's identities (both in their own minds and in the minds of others) are bound up more intricately in the decisions they make: their lifestyle choices (downtown or exurb?), their consumer behaviour (Hummer or Prius?), and, yes, their political behaviour. These choices, particularly in America, have huge symbolic resonance: they tell everyone who you are.

Progressive writer Naomi Klein believes that the Republican Party has succeeded in introducing "identity branding" into the political sphere. "[The Republicans are] not selling a product," Klein says, "they're selling a desired identity, an aspirational identity of the people who consume their product. Nike understands that, Apple understands that, and so do all the successful brands. Karl Rove understands that too." Klein points to this shift as one reason for the more rancorous political climate in the United States these days. "When George Bush's policies are attacked, rather than being dissuaded from being Republicans, Republicans feel attacked personally—because it's *your* politics. Republicanism has merged with their identity."[1]

I would argue that the increased emphasis on "values" (however amorphously defined) across the political arena is rooted in strategists' sense that Klein is right: politics have become more personal. They may not identify the phenomenon exactly as Klein does, as the success of corporate marketing in the political arena. But when they talk about "speaking to people's values" it's a kind of shorthand for political messaging in this new atmosphere Klein has described so sharply— where Americans' political affiliations have become more intensely personal, part of their psychological, emotional, and in many cases spiritual identities.

Values certainly aren't the only ingredients in people's political decisions; electoral choices are complex and can be influenced by a host of factors. Sometimes policies can do it—a whole slate of policies or even individual ones. Many religious Americans, for example, are single-issue voters: a party's policy on abortion may well be the make-or-break question.

And of course, a charismatic (or dull) candidate can all but overshadow his or her policies. Bill Clinton's charisma was famous. Many Americans' sense that he understood them, was one of them, and "felt their pain" was profound. Renowned African-American author Toni Morrison even went so far as to call Clinton "our first black President. Blacker than any actual black person who could ever be elected in our children's lifetime. After all, Clinton displays almost every trope of blackness: single-parent household, born poor, working-class, saxophone-playing, McDonald's-and-junk-food-loving boy from Arkansas."[2] Our first black president. Beat *that* with a policy paper on farm subsidies.

Beyond the policies and candidates, the vagaries of the campaign trail can exert massive influence. The famous 1988 "Willie Horton" ad—which informed Americans of a crime spree by a convicted murderer who was released from prison on a weekend pass despite having been sentenced for life without parole, all under Michael Dukakis's gubernatorial watch—arguably sank that man's presidential bid (Dukakis's, not Horton's). But perhaps the spectacle of Dukakis riding in a tank (to toughen up his image) and looking ridiculous was the final nail in the coffin of his campaign. The right ad and the wrong stunt, or vice versa, can make all the difference. And perhaps, the moment John Kerry marched on stage at the Democratic convention, saluted, and "reported for duty" was the very moment his war record became not an unassailable credential but a belaboured trick. As soon as it became a campaign performance rather than a sober chapter in Kerry's past, it became vulnerable to all the mockery Republican campaigners could hurl at it. And hurl they did: many delegates to the Republican convention could be spotted wearing Band-Aids with little purple hearts on them, allusions to Kerry's war wounds, which, amazingly, became grounds for open derision among all those Republican hawks whose SUVs surely bear "Support Our Troops" bumper stickers.

And then there's long-term history to consider. After all, until the Civil Rights Act alienated them in the 1960s, many white Southerners voted Democrat because they were still angry at the party of Lincoln over the Civil War nearly a century earlier.

Bearing in mind this complexity, it's instructive to think about how the political strategies of America's two major parties might be influenced by an empirical understanding of their constituents' (and potential constituents') values. It's particularly useful at a time when politics is so personal and values are playing such a crucial role in electoral choice. What are the values of each party's true believers? And what are the values of those coveted swing voters? Which common values can be activated by a savvy candidate, and which values will drive a damaging wedge between the core and the fence-sitters?

DEFINING PROGRESSIVES AND CONSERVATIVES

We've used our data to formulate profiles of politically engaged Americans across the political spectrum in order to see how ardent progressives and conservatives might speak to their "constituencies of opportunity" most effectively using the language of values. In order to see how true believers on each side might best communicate with moderates, we of course had to define those true believers. We chose a fairly arbitrary cut-off of 20 percent—that is, we isolated the one-fifth of Certain Voters most committed to one side or the other (20 percent Republican, 20 percent Democrat)—and created profiles of their values.[3] We then went beyond the two cores and found the moderates, selecting the next 31 percent that each group would need to gain a majority of the popular vote and examining those groups' values. (Of course, the two moderate groups overlap by 2 percent in the middle, since either side would need a majority to win.)

How, then, did we define these groups of progressives and conservatives? In our surveys, we ask all respondents a number of questions associated with politics. We ask them about their ideological orientation (liberal or conservative), their party affiliation (Democrat, Republican, Independent), and their presidential candidate preference for the year of the survey (it's fortuitous that our U.S. surveys, conducted every four years, fall in the summer prior to presidential elections). We also ask respondents about a handful of issues that tend to correlate with political orientation: public health care, the right to own firearms without a licence, abortion, the privatization of government services, taxes, and welfare.

When we set out to categorize Americans into core progressives, moderate progressives, moderate conservatives, and core conservatives, we had a number of options as to how to define these groups. One option was to establish a spectrum based on one or more of the categories listed above. For example, we could take people who identified as strong Democrats *and* strong liberals and put them at one end of the scale, put those who said they were strong conservatives *and* strong Republicans at the other end, and use some system to plot others at points in between (those who were moderate conservatives but strong Republicans, or moderate Democrats but strong liberals, and all the other gradations). We could then mark our cut-off points to establish a "core" of about 20 percent on either end and the roughly 31 percent each core group would require to gain a majority of popular support.

Ultimately, however, we found that it was two *different* measures that yielded the best portraits of core conservatives and core progressives. That is, the most coherent and intuitively valid groups emerged when we used different criteria to isolate progressives and conservatives rather than plotting respondents along a single spectrum.

Here, I'll just deal with the one most obvious concern that arises from this approach. A skeptic might well ask, "Have you not just isolated progressives and conservatives using criteria that yield the values profiles that best accord with your preconceptions about how progressives and conservatives think?"

Yes and no—but mainly no. First of all, by any definition—conservative versus liberal, Republican versus Democrat, Bush versus Kerry, or issue-based definitions (abortion, taxation, and so on)—conservatives and progressives emerge with values profiles that to a greater or lesser extent accord with those I'm about to explain. People who told us they planned to vote for Bush don't look vastly different from people who say they're strong Republicans, for example. There are shades of difference, yes, which is why we ask so many discrete questions about politics instead of just assuming that Bush voters are Republicans are conservatives are pro-gun people, and so on. But there are significant areas of overlap. So our challenge was not to formulate values profiles that fit all our assumptions or that demonized one side or the other, but to arrive at profiles that were internally consistent and that hung together to form some kind of world view we could recognize as existing in the American political landscape.

So yes: we wanted to look at the values and say, "I've seen this represented at party conventions and in political ads and person-on-the-street interviews. This mindset seems to exist in the world." To that extent, we were looking for what we wanted to find. We would have been wary, for example, of a values profile of Bush voters that found them to be strongly secular, strongly in favour of gay rights, and extremely weak on patriotism. But we certainly didn't look to find good guys and bad guys.

It is my hope that both progressives and conservatives will recognize themselves in the values profiles I will describe, and that neither will feel maligned or misrepresented. We didn't set out to show that liberals are defined by spinelessness and conservatives by bigotry or anything of the kind; we set out to learn more about the fundamental values that underpin the opinions that each side expresses. Hence, we looked for values that match those opinions and policies.

So what definitions did we end up using? Interestingly enough, we arrived at the most robust profile of liberals when we used issues to define them. We asked our respondents to agree or disagree with the following six statements on a four-point scale.

1. All Americans should have comprehensive health care coverage regardless of their ability to pay for it.
2. I support the right to own firearms, including automatic weapons, without a licence.
3. I believe that abortion is murder.
4. America should privatize as many government services as possible.
5. Taxes are too high. I'll vote against any increase in taxes.
6. Welfare and other social programs don't help poor people. They just breed dependency on the government.

When we created a spectrum that ranged from people who landed on the "progressive" side of all six issues to those who landed on the "conservative" side of all six, we found that the progressive side looked both coherent and intuitive. People with progressive values seemed to cohere strongly around this selection of issues. So we took the roughly 20 percent nearest the progressive pole of the spectrum (about 20 percent of respondents were progressive on five or six of the issues) and examined them as "core progressives": the true believers who form the base of progressive politics in the United States. We then examined the next 31 percent: the group in the next segment of the spectrum to whom the core progressives must speak in order to achieve electoral success.

This spectrum that revealed such a crisp and intuitive picture of progressives, however, yielded a strange picture of people on the other, conservative side of the six issues. They looked nothing like the conservatives we see in American electoral politics. Indeed, they didn't look conservative at all: they looked reckless, hedonistic, exceedingly materialistic, and more secular than progressives. So we began to seek other ways of looking at conservatives.

As it turned out, the most convincing portrait of conservatives emerged when we measured not their positions on issues but their self-identification as conservatives. To find our core conservatives, we took people who identified themselves as both strong conservatives and strong Republicans and looked at their values. There were, we discovered, fifteen key values that differentiated these people from other politically engaged Americans. So the group we've labelled "core conservatives" are the 20 percent of politically engaged Americans who are strongest on those fifteen values. Our "moderate conservatives" are the next 31 percent along the spectrum.

Initially, it seemed puzzling that we couldn't fit liberals and conservatives on the same spectrum. Most people are used to thinking in political binaries that are variations of the right wing/left wing dichotomy. But ultimately it makes great sense that this dichotomy didn't fit: it's by now practically a truism of American politics that liberals have issues while conservatives have values. So it's fascinating, and in its way (with 20/20 hindsight) predictable, that in our analysis, liberals should cohere around issues and conservatives around values.

This result also jells with our finding, discussed in Chapter 2, that liberals and conservatives are not as diametrically opposed as political rhetoric would often suggest. As politically engaged Americans, liberals and conservatives share considerable common ground and are much less different from each other than they are from the politically disengaged. So perhaps we shouldn't be surprised that we don't find them shouting at each other across vast gulfs of disagreement (from opposing ends of a single spectrum) but rather simply congregating around different *kinds* of ideas, defined not necessarily by distaste for each other's ideas but by distinct language and thinking that doesn't always translate.

Our values profiles of progressives and conservatives, and of the moderates who lean in one direction or the other, show some intuitive, even stereotypical differences between true believers and moderates on both sides, and also some surprising sites of agreement.

PROGRESSIVES

The 20 Percent Core: True Believers

According to an observation often attributed to Winston Churchill, anyone who's not a liberal at age twenty-five has no heart and anyone who's not a conservative by age thirty-five has no brain. When we define a core progressive camp in the United States based on the above criteria and generate its profile, the values that emerge do indeed centre to a great extent on the heart: progressives are especially strong on values associated with empathy and fairness and with interpersonal connection and engagement. Their empathy leads to an inclusive mindset that underlies their commitment to flexibility and diversity.

When measured against other Certain Voters, the progressives are vastly above average on *Flexible Families* and *Flexible Gender Identity,* both trends that suggest a desire to define one's identity and family according to one's own needs and feelings rather than in a manner prescribed by institutions or social convention.

This flexibility is intimately linked to their approach to spirituality. American progressives are strong on *Religion à la Carte* and *Spiritual Quest,* indicating a belief that one's spiritual life must be pursued in the way one finds most meaningful *personally;* the quest for meaning may involve portions of numerous philosophies and faith traditions, and not be adopted whole hog, as orthodox versions of most faiths would insist (since most faiths have a built-in concept of their own truth and infallibility). Picture a cultural Catholic who practises birth control, believes women should be allowed to be priests, loved Dan Brown's *Da Vinci Code,* and thinks Zen Buddhism is cool.

This flexibility also applies to matters racial and cultural: progressives are well above the average among Certain Voters on the trends *Racial Fusion* and *Culture Sampling.* These Americans are comfortable with the idea of racial mixing, not only casual social mixing (*Culture Sampling* deals primarily with learning from people of different backgrounds and having a diverse group of friends) but mixing in the form of intermarriage. If a progressive white Protestant couple's son brought home for dinner a young woman he met in his MBA program at Harvard whose parents lived in New Delhi and were practising Hindus, they'd take it as a sign of their success in raising a cosmopolitan individual—not as an affront to their own background. All this flexibility likely flows from a strong need for autonomy, which this group articulates in part in its high score on *Personal Control.* Not surprisingly, core progressives are strong on *Rejection of Authority* and *Rejection of Order* and weak on *Patriarchy.*

American progressives stand out from Certain Voters at large in their commitment to fairness and equality: they are well above average on the trend *Social Responsibility,* reporting a sense of personal obligation to help people less fortunate than themselves, and the belief that people should work together to solve social problems. Progressives also score high on *Largesse Oblige,* the belief that the rich have a moral duty to help the poor. They are equally intent on equality among people of different races and genders, scoring high on *Gender Parity* and *Acknowledgment of Racism.* Finally, progressives register a willingness to put their principles into action, reporting that they try to take the ethics of the companies they support into account when they make purchases *(Ethical Consumerism)* and that they try to remain connected with political happenings and perform such civic duties as voting and jury duty *(Civic Engagement).* The single strongest value for this segment is *Ecological Concern.*

Some of the focus on fairness we find in the values of core progressives may come from the fact that these Americans are so interested in engaging emotionally with others. They score well above the average Certain Voter on the trend *Introspection and Empathy,* reporting that they try to look at their own souls in the mirror, put themselves in the shoes of those with whom they disagree, and, more broadly, are interested in trying to understand their society. Whereas some people may feel guilty when walking past a panhandler without giving him any money, the most devout among core progressives will give him money and *still* feel guilty for not having taken time to have a coffee and a chat—acknowledging the panhandler's humanity and shoring up their own. For these Americans, emotional generosity and material generosity cannot be disentangled.

Progressives say it's important to them to savour little day-to-day pleasures and to be able to take time out of their routine when they're needed by people close to them. And it's not just for emergencies that they'll deviate from their routines. Core progressives say they like to spice up their lives by being spontaneous. For these Americans, spontaneity is one key to authenticity.

Many of the foregoing trends are inner-directed—they rely on a quest for meaning and fulfillment that one defines personally rather than adhering to a code dictated by society or an institution like a church. And an important aspect of progressives' inner-directedness is their rejection of consumption; we find an exceptional indifference to material goods that might impress others and a lack of enthusiasm about shopping for those goods.[4] Core progressives are strong on *Discriminating Consumerism* (they try to make informed consumption choices and resist impulse buying) and *Skepticism Toward Advertising,* and weak on *Joy of Consumption, Importance of Brand, Crude Materialism,* and *Ostentatious Consumption.* They also register little *Need for Status Recognition,* which in the American context means they're more likely to derive self-esteem from experience than from material possessions. These are America's quintessential postmaterial postmoderns.

Of course, the language we use to describe world views is loaded. What I term flexibility many conservatives would call moral laxity. What I call fairness many conservatives would see as reverse discrimination, citing what they consider to be the excesses of feminism, affirmative action, and political correctness. What I call inner-directedness many conservatives would call selfishness or narcissism: a refusal to adhere to generally accepted social codes of morality, decency, and responsibility. But however one interprets the values I've described, I hope progressives will recognize themselves in the profile, and I suspect conservatives will recognize progressives. It's remarkable that a group defined by answers to six questions on such apparently disparate topics should adhere so strongly to such a coherent and recognizable set of values.

THE NEXT 31 PERCENT: MODERATES AND SWINGERS

Having defined our progressive true believers, the 20 percent of Certain Voters who are most progressive on our six selected issues, let's now look at the next most progressive 31 percent of Certain Voters and where their values match—and differ from—the core group. These are the moderates to whom progressives must reach out in their policies and messaging as they seek to make political gains both in electoral politics and through progressive foundations and charities, NGOs, and other political projects outside the voting booth.

On the values associated with flexibility and diversity, core and moderate progressives overlap partially. Moderates, like the core, are strong on values associated with racial and ethnic diversity: they have above average scores on *Racial Fusion* and *Culture Sampling* and, like the core, strongly reject *Xenophobia*. There's room for people and, more particularly, *practices* from all over the world in moderate progressives' America.

This flexibility extends to the family to some extent. Like core progressives, moderates score above the average among Certain Voters on *Flexible Families*—but nowhere near as high. They might not disown a gay son, but they'd be more comfortable if he came home with Eve rather than Steve. Moderates also accord with core progressives in their rejection of the idea that the father of the family must rule the roost *(Patriarchy)*; the entire progressive side of the spectrum seems to agree on egalitarianism in the family and even diverse family models. But moderates reject the core progressives' concept of *Flexible Gender Identity*. For them, men should still be men and women should still be women, but maybe the country won't crumble if a few of these men and women combine in non-traditional ways.

Moderate progressives, for example, might be less sympathetic than the core to some would-be female firefighters' pleas for physical try-outs that take into account women's lesser average muscle mass. Perhaps, moderates may reason, the job is just meant for one of those brawny heroes we imagine doing endless bench presses in the firehouse with the boys. If a woman can pass the chin-up test, terrific. If not, maybe she should find a gig that has different requirements. (Moderately progressive Americans, however, would be careful not to append "dear" or "sweetheart" to this advice.)

Although moderate progressives agree that people should be able to construct their families in their own ways, this belief seems to flow more from tolerance than from a rejection of the rules that have traditionally defined family: moderates are about average on the value *Rejection of Authority,* while core progressives are very high. Moreover, moderate progressives are more likely to feel some religious push in the direction of the traditional family (even if they question or reject that particular edict), since they're more likely to adhere to a coherent, institutional faith. Unlike the core, moderates register little interest in defining religion on their own terms; they're average on *Spiritual Quest,* while core progressives are strong. Moderates take an even dimmer view of mixing and matching beliefs and practices: they are extremely weak on *Religion à la Carte,* whereas the core are exceptionally strong (in fact, *Religion à la Carte* marks the single greatest divergence between core and moderate progressives). The value *Religiosity* is the mirror image of this phenomenon, with moderates being stronger than average and the core being weaker than average.

Folk musician Arlo Guthrie tells a story about the day he was born. The nurse who was responsible for gathering information for his birth certificate asked his mother what religion she should put down on the form. "None," the mother replied. The nurse told her she couldn't put "none" (this was 1947). "Well then, put 'all,'" the tired mother said. The nurse figured she was dealing with an eccentric and decided to wait for the baby's father, famous folkie Woody Guthrie. When Guthrie rushed into the hospital to see his new son and was asked what religion the nurse should mark in the box, he said, "Put 'none.'" Told with some exasperation that this was impossible, he paused and suggested, "Well then, put 'all.'" Moderate progressives seem to hold similar views about religion, although not as approvingly as the Guthries: if you're going to take bits and pieces of everything, you might as well not take anything. Religions are complete systems; you either sign on for the full monty or you don't. Moderate progressives may not be fundamentalists, but, quite simply, they believe in and play by the rules. This is one of their key differences from the more flexible and syncretic core progressives.

Moderates, like the core, are highly engaged with society: they're above average even when compared with other Certain Voters (an engaged bunch) on the trend *Civic Engagement*. But moderates and core progressives differ somewhat in their understanding of how American society is working and what wrongs need (or don't need) to be righted. Moderates agree that men and women should be treated equally *(Gender Parity)*, and, like core progressives, they score very low on the trend *Modern Racism,* disagreeing with such statements as "Over the past few years, African Americans have gained more economically than they deserve."

When it comes to economic inequality and the redistribution of income, though, moderates diverge sharply from core progressives by scoring below average on *Social Responsibility* and *Largesse Oblige*. This greater skepticism about redistributive approaches to poverty is likely underpinned by moderates' greater confidence that a level playing field exists in contemporary America. They score much higher than core progressives on belief in the *American Dream,* the belief that with hard work, anyone can still make it in America regardless of his or her background. Moderates also score lower than core progressives on the trend *Acknowledgment of Racism,* being less likely to agree with such statements as "In American society, whites have an unfair advantage." So while they're not resentful of the ground that African Americans, for example, have gained through programs like affirmative action, they're more likely than core progressives to believe that the wrongs of history have largely been righted and that all Americans, regardless of race, probably get a fair shake these days.

Although moderate progressives share core progressives' high level of *Ecological Concern,* they're less likely to say that they'd avoid actually buying products from companies whose practices damage the environment. Indeed, moderates score much lower overall on the trend *Ethical Consumerism,* expressing less willingness than core progressives to put their money where their values are when they shop. This difference may derive in part from the fact that moderates simply don't have the flexibility to spend more on fair trade, shade-grown coffee or union-made golf shirts: moderates far outstrip core progressives on the trend *Discount Consumerism,* suggesting that they're looking for low prices first and foremost. As for the other consumption-related trends on which core progressives score so low, moderates are equally indifferent: they have low scores on *Joy of Consumption, Buying on Impulse, Ostentatious Consumption,* and *Need for Status Recognition.* There is little interest in ostentation here, whether it means showing off the flashiest toy or the most virtuous dish detergent.

This seems to me a fairly intuitive portrait of moderate progressives. They are somewhat more traditional than core progressives, favouring institutional religion over postmodern "spiritual quests" but incorporating modern social tolerance with standard religious practice. Moderates broadly favour equality and the advances women and racial minorities have made in the past several decades, but they believe that America today is essentially a fair place and a land of opportunity for everyone. They're more reluctant than core progressives to agree, for example, that "If an African American doesn't succeed, it's more likely to be because of society than because of the shortcomings of the individual." Finally, moderates are less likely to incorporate their progressivism into all aspects of their identity, up to and including consumption choices: these Americans believe that workers should be treated fairly and the environment protected, but they're not about to boycott Wal-Mart for disallowing unions (incidentally, moderates are stronger than cores on *Confidence in Big Business*). They may take their politics to the voting booth but not necessarily to the cash register.

CONSERVATIVES

THE 20 PERCENT CORE: TRUE BELIEVERS

When we look at the values of core conservatives, a portrait emerges that's familiar without being stereotypical. The Americans we identify as being among the most conservative 20 percent espouse values oriented toward tradition, authority, and patriotism. They also have strong faith in American institutions, from the traditional family to the large businesses (corporate institutions, one might say) that have been nurtured by the American marketplace.

In his first campaign for Senate, Texas Republican Phil Gramm made an oft-quoted remark that is emblematic of the unwaveringly positive take many conservatives tend to have on America, warts (beauty marks?) and all. Explaining that America can't be as beset by inequality and hidden poverty as critics claim, Gramm asked, "Has anyone ever noticed that we live in the only country in the world where all the poor people are fat?" Of course, many liberals tend to cast obesity among the poor as an epidemic visited upon them by cynical fast-food chains that prey upon two poverties—little money and little time—to reap huge profits on fatty, nutritionally bankrupt food, thus saddling their customers with spiralling health problems. What a different perspective Gramm takes on the issue: you're lucky to live in America, where you have a chance to get fat!

The core group of American conservatives we've identified is, as many of their political representatives attest, traditional and religious. Politically engaged Americans are more religious than the general population, and politically engaged *conservatives* are more religious still. Core conservatives are more likely to believe passionately in a rigid and unchanging definition of the family. Moreover, they see any slippage in gender roles as the seed of a threat to this family model.

A look at the dress codes of America's Christian universities speaks to this insistence on strictly maintained gender binaries. Bob Jones University, for example, regulates gender down to the minutest details, sensing, perhaps, that the chute from unconventional dress to homosexuality to the implosion of society is well greased and always beckoning the unwary. ("Why don't you slip on a Birkenstock, Mary?" "Robert, some highlights would really add some zest to your look.") The dress code for women at Bob Jones University includes proscriptions against pants as well as "combat boots, hiking boots, or shoes that give this appearance," and young ladies are advised to "avoid ... [hair]cuts so short that they take on a masculine look." For their part, men may not colour or highlight their hair, and jewellery other than rings (presumably only a wedding band or a Bob Jones class ring is appropriate) is forbidden.

Adherence to strict ideas about family and gender is just one facet of American conservatives' commitment to order: this group's values reveal a strong focus on hierarchy, rules, and authority. Core conservatives believe strongly in the importance of *Duty*, and they're more likely to automatically obey and respect authority figures *(Obedience to Authority)*, especially family patriarchs. This spirit of deference extends to the state, with core conservatives scoring higher on the value *National Pride* than other politically engaged Americans—and vastly higher than Americans at large. (This patriotism likely drives core conservatives' high scores on *Cultural Assimilation;* America is the greatest country on earth, and immigrants will be well served by blending in as quickly as possible. And belief in the greatness—and righteousness—of America can turn at its edges to *Xenophobia;* core conservatives are stronger on this value than other voters.)

In the values system of core conservatives, order must reign not just in the social sphere but in the emotional sphere as well: these Americans place particular emphasis on controlling their own emotions (the value *Emotional Control*). Another manifestation of this commitment to order and appropriateness is their emphasis on appropriate dress and behaviour *(Propriety)*. Think of the military mentality, in which mirror-like boots and properly creased pants symbolize so much about an individual's ability to do precisely what's expected of him, to register respect for others through his physical appearance, and to fit seamlessly into a larger system.

Another set of values that distinguishes core conservatives from other voters revolves around the idea that America lives up to its ideals as a land of fairness, opportunity, and meritocracy. Chief among these values is, of course, the *American Dream*. Core conservatives are much more likely than other voters to profess faith that anyone who works hard can still make it in America. The corollary is that those who meet with failure have brought it on themselves. Core conservatives score high on *Just Deserts,* the belief that misfortune is usually earned just as much as success is. And if those who make it deserve everything they've got, then businesses that make it must be equally virtuous: core conservatives score high on *Confidence in Big Business,* believing that large businesses usually function well and strike a fair balance between profits and the public interest. Having succeeded and flourished in the free and fair market, big businesses are naturally more trustworthy than government, and core conservatives would like to see business exert greater influence in society *(More Power for Business).* And of course those virtuous, successful businesses wouldn't lie to Americans about their products: these core conservatives are distinguished from other voters by their *Confidence in Advertising.*

The values profile of America's core conservatives jells well with conservative politics in the United States. The mindset here is sober, culturally conservative, pro-business, and deeply patriotic—with patriotism implying a belief not just in the righteousness of America's ideals but that America is successfully living up to those ideals. I hope readers will recognize the party faithful in this values profile; to me, these values are plainly evident in the Republican Party's candidates, policies, and public statements. But what of the people who are a less seamless fit with party ideology—those who consider themselves conservative but aren't part of that unwavering 20 percent of voters who have come to be known as "The Base"?

THE NEXT 31 PERCENT: MODERATES AND SWINGERS

Reflecting on the Republican Convention held in September 2004 in New York City, Hendrik Hertzberg mused in *The New Yorker* that "moderation" seemed to be at least a putative theme of the event. After a first term of aggressively rolling back environmental regulations in favour of business (including advocating drilling in the Arctic National Wildlife Refuge), enacting what even some right-wingers have called "big-brother conservatism" under Attorney General John Ashcroft (who used the Patriot Act to gain access to the medical records of women who had obtained late-term abortions, presumably just in case they posed a threat to homeland security), and cozying up to religious conservatives by curbing funding for stem cell research and proposing a constitutional amendment prohibiting same-sex marriage, one might be forgiven for asking whether the executive branch under Bush really prizes moderation. Hertzberg wrote,

> Moderate politicians were used at this Republican convention the way people of color were used at the last one: as props. McCain, Giuliani, Schwarzenegger, and the rest were allowed to show themselves. They were allowed to praise Bush and ... to attack Kerry, and they were allowed to recommend civility ... But none of them said a word about the social and environmental issues that mark them as moderates. If 2000 was minstrelsy, this was mime.

Is it true that moderates are being denied a voice in the Republican Party—not just literally silenced in that most public forum, the pre-election convention, but also more generally ignored in the offices and meeting rooms where decisions are made? Or is the party simply representing the ideas and ideals of American conservatives at large during a trying period in U.S. history? In order to understand whether the Republican Party is adequately representing or dangerously alienating its more moderate members (an error from which the Democratic Party has yet to recover), it is worth taking a look at people whose values mark them as conservative but who stand somewhat apart from the core conservatives we've examined earlier in this chapter.

In our analysis, moderate American conservatives emerge as notably skeptical of both core conservative and core progressive ideology. Rejecting much of the traditionalism and ardent patriotism of core conservatives, and also showing a distinct lack of enthusiasm for the egalitarianism and inclusivity prized by core progressives, moderate progressives are perhaps the most individualistic segment in our analysis.

While core conservatives score well above average on values like *Religiosity, Propriety,* and *Duty,* moderate conservatives are below average. With a less traditional and religious outlook on life, moderates are not as worried about the preservation of the *Traditional Family* or *Traditional Gender Identity* as core conservatives are. (This is not to say that moderate conservatives are out campaigning for gay rights; they score low on *Flexible Families.* But it may be that anti-same-sex marriage ballot measures, for example, won't be as effective in getting moderates to the polls in support of the Republicans as in drawing out more ardent and religious conservatives.)

Moderate conservatives diverge sharply from core conservatives on patriotism-oriented values, including *National Pride* and *American Dream*. Not only do moderates see their personal identities as less bound up in their identity as Americans than core conservatives do, moderates express somewhat less faith in one of the pillars of American life: the American Dream. Whereas *American Dream* is among the values that most strongly define core conservatives, moderate conservatives are below average among Certain Voters on this trend.

Moderate conservatives score below average on some of the old-fashioned salt-of-the-earth values embraced by core conservatives; moderates are below average among Certain Voters on both *Everyday Ethics* and *Work Ethic,* for example. On the other hand, moderates also steer clear of some of the harder edges of the world view we find among core conservatives, including values like *Xenophobia* and *Sexism*. (Again, core conservatives are not defined by these "hard edges," but they do score higher than the average Certain Voter on these values, whereas moderates are slightly below average.)

Xenophobia is an area in which Republican leaders have had to tread very carefully over the past several years: they have waged war in two predominantly Muslim countries but stressed that the war on terror is not a war against Muslims. President Bush has invited Muslim clerics for Ramadan dinners at the White House, has repeatedly praised Islam as a religion of peace, and has admonished his citizens against blaming ordinary Muslims or Arab Americans for the 9/11 attacks. This behaviour may be aimed partly at hearts and minds in the Islamic world; America's terrorist foes would likely be thrilled to see Bush cast the war on terror as a war of Christians versus Muslims, so playing down the "clash of civilizations" angle defuses that frame somewhat. But public opinion in the Muslim world is less crucial to the fate of the current administration than is public opinion at home. The hand of friendship Bush extends to Arab Americans and ordinary Muslims is certainly meant to be witnessed by American voters, especially moderate conservatives.

A handful of core conservatives probably don't mind when prominent figures in the war on terror stray slightly "off-message," as when Lieutenant General William Boykin was quoted as saying the war was a battle between Judeo-Christian values and "a guy named Satan." But the Bush White House knows this sort of rhetoric won't play with the vast majority of voters and has publicly rebuked those who overlay fiery religious themes on what is supposed to be a surgical war of self-defence.

It is not only in discussing the war zones in the Arab world that the White House treads carefully around matters of xenophobia. Republican politicians in general and the Bush administration in particular are bending over backward to court Latino voters—and that means dealing thoughtfully with Mexico and with migrant workers who cross into the United States illegally. A smart and compassionate approach to the Mexican border and "illegals" already living and working in the U.S. should play well not just to Latinos but also to moderate conservatives.

While moderate conservatives register relatively little interest in some of the key values that distinguish core conservatives, they seem to find many of the values of core progressives equally uncompelling. They are weak on values associated with economic egalitarianism and income redistribution, such as *Social Responsibility* and *Largesse Oblige*. Just as they want other people's hands off their wallets, moderate conservatives guard their date-books with vigilance. On trends associated with community participation, moderate conservatives tend to score below average: as well as being weak on *Community Involvement,* these Americans register little desire for *Social Intimacy*. The attitude to the natural environment in this segment amounts more or less to a shrug. Moderate conservatives are even stronger than core conservatives on the value of *Ecological Fatalism*.

If moderate conservatives seem lukewarm on so many of the values of their more politically ardent compatriots, then what do they believe in? In a sense, moderate conservatives believe mainly in themselves: their values are guided primarily by their own quests for both meaning and status. They are strong, for example, on a number of values associated with status and conformity: *Need for Status Recognition, Conformity to Norms,* and *Ostentatious Consumption*.

But this attraction to status and consumption does not give way to an excessively hedonistic or aggressively competitive outlook. Moderate conservatives are strong on some values associated with interpersonal connection and quests for personal meaning. They score high on *Spiritual Quest*, for example, despite their low levels of *Religiosity*. Similarly, although they aren't as keen as core progressives on *Community Involvement*, moderate conservatives' high scores on *Personal Expression* suggest that they place considerable emphasis on cultivating meaningful and authentic relationships with those close to them, especially on being able to express themselves fully and honestly to others.

Overall, then, moderate conservatives are individualistic in their values; they are mainly preoccupied with seeking meaning as they see fit (not necessarily in the context of a religious community or even a voluntary association) and pursuing the material lifestyles they desire. They are less attracted than other politically engaged Americans to slates of values they might foster and express in a communal setting, whether with core conservatives in a religious community or with core progressives in a secular civil organization like a volunteer group or community association. But while moderate conservatives are individualistic (and more materialistic than other groups of politically engaged Americans), they are not nihilistic or hostile to their fellow citizens. They score low on *Acceptance of Violence,* and of course their civic engagement is among their defining characteristics (although their civic engagement is lower than that of other Americans who say they are certain to vote). Their values profile suggests that moderate conservatives may well be the most devout guardians of conservative individualism in America. They stand apart from core progressives, who have an explicitly communitarian streak in their values, and also from core conservatives, whose values are more heavily informed by a religious world view that entails universal codes of behaviour. Some core conservatives would like to see these codes imposed legislatively; moderate conservatives' values suggest they would surely balk at any effort in this direction.

T HESE PORTRAITS obviously belie some elements of real party politics. In the real world, few organizations if any—even those that strive toward fundamentalism—can remain ideologically pure. Concessions are inevitably made to pragmatism. On the U.S. scene, both major parties have camps whose specific agendas set them at odds with others (libertarians versus social conservatives on the Republican side, for example, and environmentalists versus unions on the Democrat side). The agendas of both parties are internally inconsistent: whereas Republicans overall favour freedom to bear arms and make money, Democrats favour regulation in these areas. But when it comes to issues on which Republicans seek regulation on moral grounds (such as gay rights and abortion), Democrats are all for individual freedom. Nevertheless, the two parties to a greater or lesser extent manage to come together. It means something to identify as a Republican or Democrat; people don't inevitably ask "Yes, but what faction?" Our two values-based groups, which we position as the "core" of each side, are those who would likely embrace most fully the whole slate of internally inconsistent—albeit conventionally understood—principles that each party tends to stand for.

It's impossible for a recovering pollster not to reflect on what his social values data and analyses might mean for the next quadrennial presidential contest in 2008. The Republicans, who are now just barely the majority party, will of course endeavour to retain office by reassembling their majority coalition. They will wish to nominate a candidate who both consolidates the conservative base and reaches out to the 31 percent whose values are most similar to those of the core. But although the Republican coalition has been amazingly disciplined to date, there are rumblings of overreach in the party's religious wing. Their striking break with public opinion on the Terri Schiavo matter may have been a blip—or a foreshadowing of a rift between the party's more strenuous Christians and those who were happy with the results of their first birth.

The Democrats, now the "out" party and in a minority position, will be faced with another hard choice: either a candidate who can deliver red meat (or a vegan delight) to its core, virtually assuring the party, in the tradition of a Barry Goldwater in '64 or George McGovern in '72, a righteous defeat; or a candidate who can consolidate the core but also reach out to the 31 percent closest in values for a possible victory. My guess is that with Supreme Court nominations looming and the Christian right pushing further into the public domain, Democrats will be even hungrier for a win in 2008 than in 2004 and, unlike in the last presidential election, will believe that in a time of relative peace, and with no incumbent to knock off, they can do it.

It's dangerous (but fun) to speculate on personalities so far in advance in the game of politics, where a week is a lifetime and the revelation of an indiscretion, real or fabricated, can alter or even destroy an image. Still, if one reflects not only on the values profiles outlined in this chapter but also on the importance of traditional values among the engaged American public who'd be expected to vote in 2008, it wouldn't be surprising if patriarchy proved a factor in candidate selection for both parties. And in each, patriarchy suggests candidates who are beautifully situated in America's red and blue geography to bear the standard for their parties and to reach out to the potential supporters awaiting their entreaties.

For the Republicans, we have the almost too obvious choice of Jeb Bush, the current governor of Florida, the reputedly smart brother of the current president, and the son of the first George of this dynasty. Florida as home base has the advantage of being a swing state crucial (in 2000, essential) to winning the White House. He also boasts a wife of Mexican origin, a conversion to Roman Catholicism, and a long and favourable record in his home state.

The Democrats have an equally obvious choice. Someone hailing from Illinois, who spent time in Arkansas and now represents New York State, the bedrock of the American Democratic Party, in the nation's Senate. Her most important demographic characteristic, however, is not her regional trajectory (Midwest, Deep South, Northeast: a trifecta, George W. might say) but her gender. That's because it has enabled her to be the spouse of the most popular Democratic president since John Kennedy. Hillary Clinton can therefore tap American voters' abiding attachment to patriarchy in the manner of Indira Gandhi, whose political career was propelled forward when her widowed father served as India's prime minister. Indira ably filled the role of female companion left vacant by her deceased mother by playing domestic hostess to foreign leaders and travelling widely with her father. Between high-level exposure to the political scene and the revered family name she gained upon marrying Feroze Gandhi, Indira was twice blessed with reflected patriarchal legitimacy. Her intelligence and competence were necessary, but likely not sufficient, conditions for her election to prime ministerial office in 1967. Not to detract from her own personal qualities of leadership, but she sure had what the Brits call royal jelly.

*"In a further effort to ingratiate herself with New Yorkers,
Hillary Clinton threw out the first pitch at last night's Yankee game
and went on to pitch three scoreless innings."*

While not quite up to the Kennedy standard, the Clintons are as close to royalty as the Democrats can offer Americans this decade, and what they lack in pedigree they make up for in celebrity and charisma. With her own intelligence and magnetism at work, and with the bonus of Big Bill applauding proudly near the podium, Hillary Clinton has an excellent shot at gaining the approval of both the you-go-girl crowd and the any-friend-of-Bill's set. And one never knows: secret ballots mean some American women may just make a quiet pact with Hillary in the voting booth before rejoining their Republican husbands in the SUV.

The face-off between these two American dynasties from a socio-cultural perspective seems almost inevitable—Bush versus Clinton redux. It makes sense that in a country whose wealthy elite are differentiated from their fellows in a way not seen since the Gilded Age over a century and a quarter ago, and at a time of increasingly Darwinist economic struggle and manic worship of celebrity, the contest of iconic leaders for the prerogatives and spoils of presidential office is all but written in stone. Americans may love an underdog, but these days he shouldn't be so far under that no one's ever heard of him (as Arnold "Total Recall" Schwarzenegger might attest).

The choice of presidential running mates is usually a footnote to the main race. Still, the sight of Secretary of State Rice standing on the podium to accept the Republican nomination for vice-president, the first African American on the ticket of the party of Abraham Lincoln *and* the first woman (take that, Hillary), would be a cool move. As she seeks a running mate, Senator Clinton will *not* be in search of cool, as she has more than cornered that quality herself ... she's so cool she's hot. Hers will be the prosaic selection of a regional balance to her New York base—she'll need on her ticket a Real Man with gravitas (no women need apply, even from California) to serve as her avuncular Dick Cheney, and if, like New Mexico governor Bill Richardson, this real man can also boast some Latino heritage, so much the better. Barak Obama, the dashing, smart, and eloquent hit of the 2004 Democratic convention, may have to spend a little more time on the vine before a bid for higher office.

I end my book with such speculation if only to convey that my report on this research is intended not just to enlighten but perhaps even *lighten* the discussion of social change in America, which from my perch atop Toronto's CN Tower seems all too mean and divisive, albeit exciting. The culture war over values in America, as my analysis shows, is overblown; the so-called red and blue Americas have a lot more in common with each other than they do with the plurality of Americans who are disengaged from their political system. And while the core conservatives and the core liberals yelling at each other seem to have little common ground other than the blessed geography they share on the North American continent, the diverse "constituencies of opportunity" that lie beyond these two ideological camps do not ground their perspectives on public life in hatred of one another. They will, as always, base their vote choices on hope, aspiration, and decency … unless fate dictates that the politics of fear will escalate with, heaven forbid, further terrorist attacks and/or ongoing war. But even in this terrible instance, George W. Bush is constrained from running for re-election, so the country will be forced to choose a new commander-in-chief from a list of civilians. Generals who so dominated the office from Washington to Eisenhower (a total of twelve occupied the Oval Office in that time) have been largely peripheral since then. The most obvious military man on offer—an intelligent, charismatic, and highly competent former general, a former secretary of state, and an African American to boot—would probably be less hawkish than most civilian Republican candidates (and he would probably not be spotted wearing a purple heart Band-Aid). And in any case, Colin Powell may be enjoying a lower-profile existence, golfing, fishing, baking, meditating, or writing a sweeping memoir of his years in uniform and in the halls of worldly power.

Of course, whomever the parties nominate and whoever ends up being inaugurated president in January 2009 will be trying to unite a nation divided on the question of American values and how to achieve them (whatever they are) at home and abroad. America has been divided before, never more so, of course, than in the 1860s when the nation was embroiled in a bloody civil war. America has also been united, or at least not as acrimoniously divided, under Franklin Roosevelt, Ronald Reagan, and briefly under John Kennedy.

Kennedy remains a fascinating political icon for the American people, chosen in our 2004 survey as the public person, living or dead, whom citizens admire the most. We didn't offer a list of potential candidates; Americans had to write in their own heroes, and Kennedy appeared most frequently. In this he surprisingly eclipses Washington, Jefferson, Lincoln,

FDR, and even Ronald Reagan, the political father of modern conservatism in America. I suspect Kennedy is admired not for his substantive accomplishments but for his sophisticated style, for his wit, and for the values he so eloquently espoused. With the able assistance of his speechwriter, Ted Sorenson, Kennedy promised in his inaugural address to represent a new generation of Americans "born in this century, tempered by war, disciplined by a hard and bitter peace, proud of our ancient heritage" and asked his fellow Americans to express their patriotism not in war but in peaceful internationalism, including a commitment to the United Nations, "our last best hope."

But Kennedy was no wimp. In that memorable speech he announced, "Let every nation know, whether it wishes us well or ill, that we shall pay any price, bear any burden, meet any hardship, support any friend, oppose any foe, in order to assure the survival and the success of liberty." A few months later he acted on those words by going to the wall with Nikita Krushchev over the Soviet leader's threatened missile deployment in Cuba and forcing America's Cold War adversary to back down without bloodshed. In response to another Russian challenge, he committed America to putting a man on the moon by the end of the decade … a mission that would be accomplished by heroic American astronauts in 1969 when Neil Armstrong made that "one small step for man, one giant leap for mankind." (And, Armstrong refrained from suggesting, an especially enormous leap for those on the right side of the Iron Curtain.)

Kennedy, with his simultaneous manly gravitas (don't mess with America) and boyish aspiration (to the moon!), was able to articulate American strength and American idealism at the same time. In today's political lexicon, one might say he knew how to use language to frame the debate—an art lost by subsequent Democratic presidential hopefuls, with the exception of Bill Clinton. Most important, Kennedy was an optimist imploring his country to move forward with vigour, as he would say, to create a better world. Ronald Reagan was also an optimist and is to Republicans and conservatives what Kennedy is to Democrats and liberals. These men are the standard against which their successors will be judged.

In this book I have argued that the American electorate remains more united in their values than much public discourse would suggest. While America's leaders are currently mired in partisanship (one poll amusingly found that 50 percent of Americans see George W. Bush as a uniter while 50 percent see him as a divider), the values landscape our research reveals suggests that it's possible for a new leader to emerge who might equal or eclipse the symbolic status of Kennedy, Reagan, or even both. This leader's most powerful tool would be an inspiring national project that, like the space program in its infancy, transcends the ideological tug of war and inspires Americans to meet, together, yet another morning in their great country.

Social Values Methodology

IN THIS APPENDIX we spend some time, for the benefit of the interested reader or social researcher, detailing the social science–based theory and methodologies employed in our syndicated study of social values in America and in other countries around the world. We describe the theoretical and historical context for the emergence of social values research as a discipline, how social values are formed and evolve within both the life of the individual and that of a society, and the ten basic methodological steps we use to create structural and dynamic mappings of the social values of any society and how they're changing.

THE THEORETICAL FOUNDATIONS OF SOCIAL VALUES RESEARCH

The roots of our measurement system go back more than a century and a half to a curious young Frenchman named Alexis de Tocqueville. Tocqueville visited the United States in the 1830s in order to examine, first-hand, the social and political life of the world's "first new nation." His *Democracy in America* is to social values research what Adam Smith's *The Wealth of Nations* is to the understanding of economics. Later in the nineteenth century, economist Thorstein Veblen took another giant step forward in the description and understanding of changes to human social values with his *Theory of the Leisure Class*.

A generation ago, academic social scientists such as Maslow, Riesman, Bell, Rokeach, and Thurstone began to describe and measure social values and to explore their dynamics and impacts in contemporary societies. They also identified a hierarchy of social values. Abraham Maslow, for example, saw an evolution and structure of values—beginning with those associated with physical survival at the base level of human needs and moving on up to those associated with self-actualization at the highest intellectual and moral levels of motivation. Individuals, and even whole societies, could be roughly characterized according to this values hierarchy, depending on their predominant presenting beliefs, concerns, and practices.

In everyday parlance, the term "values" has come to take on a rich panoply of meanings and connotations, as for example the ubiquitous reference to "moral values," whose precise nature is often assumed without articulation despite its being a rather nebulous concept. However, in the 1960s psychologist Milton Rokeach first theorized about and defined social values in more denotative scientific terms as having the following properties:

- they are beliefs
- they are conceptions of, preferences for, and prescriptions about desirable modes of conduct or established orientations toward living and existence
- they are conceptions of, preferences for, and prescriptions about desirable end-states of existence and personal and social ideals

Beliefs that constitute a mode of living include such values as honesty, hard work, and even "gaming the system." End-state beliefs, on the other hand, include such values as power and influence, status, health and well-being, peace, and enlightenment.

These fundamental beliefs about the desirable means and ends of human conduct and existence are thought to be largely moulded in childhood, adolescence, and early adulthood experience. Social values are informed and shaped by a person's prevalent experiences, perceptions, and learning gleaned both in the family and in close kinship and affiliation groups, as well as by exposure to the predominant socio-historical environment and influences of the times into which a person is born, raised, and comes of age (by which we mean "reaches sentient awareness of the world").

Although once massively defined and mandated by institutions such as the church and state—as codified in long-standing accepted practices and traditions and instilled in successive generations—social values have never been as idealistic or ideological as Rokeach described them, nor have they always been the pre-eminent causes of social behaviour as he certainly implied. Rather, values can also serve, quite pragmatically and after the fact, as a person's or society's adaptation to—even justification of—current personal or cultural practices. Even the vilest of these practices—Machiavellianism, torture, the suppression of women, racial genocide, and infanticide come to mind—are more often than not framed, or even "spun," in terms of the higher-order values they serve.

And in the context of today's social scientific understanding provided by fields as diverse as sociology, linguistics, and social psychology, we also consider values to be evidence of "motivated cognition." In other words, our beliefs both determine and reflect our responses to the world as we struggle to maintain biological survival, to manage our connections with those close to us, and to achieve our species predilection toward organizing socially in hierarchical, status-defined groups. So the concept of values has gone beyond beliefs about the means and ends of living to capture the deeper motivations behind our behaviour, the tendencies of our thought and feeling—conscious and unconscious—and the interpersonal dynamics related to them.

As we peel the onion of human motivation, we see that different aspects of people's thoughts and feelings about the world are well captured by an assessment of their values. These aspects include needs, wants, and aspirations; expectancies, perceptions, and habits of thought; attitudes, judgments, and opinions; and intentions, tendencies, and actions. So values stand in as a good description for a whole host of mental, emotional, and motivational postures and preparednesses (or "sets") with which we conduct our transactions with others, with the world, and with ourselves. What our research really attempts, then, is a broadband analysis of the world views of individuals and of collectives both big and small.

THE EVOLUTION OF SOCIAL VALUES

Although shaped by his or her youthful experiences of the world, a person's social values are not unchanging things set immutably in stone. Rather, they evolve through one's lifetime, albeit usually slowly. At the psychological level they change somewhat as a function of life stage, life challenges, and significant experiences. For example, which new parents among us can deny a (formerly) uncharacteristic but extreme authoritarian impulse when confronted by a raging child? Values can also change somewhat in response to such major socio-historical events as the spread of a technology like the PC or a disease like AIDS, or as the result of insecurity born of a deep recession or the trauma of war, or in the chilling aftermath of an act of terror or a great natural disaster.

Broadly speaking, however, for most of history the pace of our cultural, technological, and spiritual change can be described only as glacial. A paradigm shift in world views happened only rarely (think agriculture, iron, Christ, Galileo, Gutenberg), and its effects played out over generations of adaptation. But in our age the development of democracy and pluralism and the corresponding decline in unbending regulation of people's world views have transformed the very character of our values, with imposed stability and homogeneity within a culture and across time giving way to flux and variability.

And now, in today's rapid world of invention and cultural convergence, knowledge is discovered so rapidly that it can double within half a generation. Youth are a constant source of new ideas and beliefs that infuse the culture and become predominant as the values of older generations wane with the death of each cohort. The main mechanism for values change at a societal level today, then, is generational replacement.

SOCIAL VALUES METHODOLOGY

The methodology employed at American Environics to unearth the rich bed of meaning carried by the construct of "values" was first developed in the 1960s in Paris by Alain de Vulpian and colleagues at his company called Cofremca. The methods were invented in response to a desire to understand the apparently spontaneous rejection of traditional values and institutions evident among many young people in French society at that time. Like their North American colleagues, notably Daniel Yankelovich, these researchers' initial understanding of the societal structuring and evolution of social values came from extensive qualitative research, primarily from in-depth one-on-one interviews. This research, conducted at the height of progressive social change, revealed new attitudes toward order, religious and secular authority, success, social status, the role of the sexes, and the place of youth in society, as well as a growing orientation toward personal autonomy, informality, and immediate gratification.

In the early 1970s, the knowledge gained from this qualitative research was used by de Vulpian to create questions and scales designed to measure the diffusion of these new values within the French culture. This was accomplished through annual quantitative surveys of representative samples of the population. Thus was born the study of "socio-cultural currents"—the evolution of social values in a culture—and the resulting "Système Cofremca de Suivi des Courants Socio-Culturels" (3SC). This system was subsequently extended beyond France into more than twenty countries in Europe and the Americas. On this side of the Atlantic, our partner polling firm CROP, based in Quebec, imported the 3SC method to Canada in 1983. And in 1992, with the help of Kaagan Research Associates, Environics Research Group began its own systematic study of American social values. Outside of academic studies such as the World Values Survey based at the University of Michigan Survey Research Center, we believe that the Social Values measurement system is the largest privately funded study of human social values currently conducted on the planet.

A Technical Look at the Social Values Map

The study of social values in any culture via survey methodologies culminates, after extensive analysis and interpretive energy, in the creation of a social values "map," a visual depiction of the structure of the predominant values of that culture. Each new social values map we create for each new culture requires about ten steps of detailed methodology leading up to a trackable quantitative analysis. While we won't go into the reasons why all these steps are necessary, nor how they're carried out using our software algorithms, we set down the steps here in general terms and describe the most important aspects in detail.

The goal of the first quantitative study in a new country is to understand the major structural relations among the values in evidence there and to create a compelling social values map describing them. As more data arrive in subsequent years, we begin to explore the currents and trajectories of values evolution in that society. Here are the necessary steps in the work-up of an initial full-bodied socio-cultural profile of a society:

1. Values consultation and sensing
2. Questionnaire construction and testing
3. Survey sampling and fielding
4. Data cleaning and treatment
5. Values exploration and extraction
6. Values indexing and reliability testing
7. Respondent classification into strong or weak expression of the values
8. Perceptual mapping and anchoring
9. Solution integration and labelling
10. Inferencing and storytelling

Step 1

Values sensing is the key to developing a socio-cultural analysis for any country, for this is where we discover what is existing and prevalent, and in later researches, what is new in a society. Through the qualitative research we routinely conduct in a given culture, we constantly seek to extract and abstract what is novel and potentially socio-culturally important in relation to that which has come before. We ask what's bubbling up from the many generative groups in the culture, from youth and new immigrant groups to emerging political or religious movements. We try to sniff out what's developing in terms of political counterculture, new ideologies, technology uptake and resistance, new social forms in the family, changing attitudes toward work, trends in popular culture and entertainment, evolving patterns of consumption, emerging preferences for travel and leisure, new aesthetic and design sensibilities, evolving food and drink preferences, and so forth.

We also conduct special studies wherein we find the opinion leaders, local experts, and market mavens at the sharp edge of the values change wedge—and then interview them in depth. We also do one-on-one interviews, web-based research, anthropological studies called everyday life researches (EDLs), and countless focus groups with both average and exceptional people. As well, we lean on our international colleagues, who also conduct this type of research worldwide, for their experiences and insights. When our preparation is complete, we sift through the findings collaboratively as a research team—with all the benefits and biases of our training as sociologists and semioticians, psychologists and marketer researchers, prognosticators and communicators.

In our "search for the new," we look for what's likely to be enduring rather than faddish in cultural evolution; current fashion and hot-this-season children's toys, for example, are not viewed as constituting what we take to be values. Plus, we look for things that are likely to have multiple manifestations in people's lives. In recent years, for example, the perceived invasiveness of employers, governments, and e-commerce marketers has led to an increasing concern for privacy that's likely to find various expressions as people assert their right to privacy across a wider spectrum of their lives. We would predict that these tendencies—already in evidence among the society's "sensitives," who are quick to read and respond to emerging social realities—have a good chance of diffusing more generally throughout the culture. But we may be wrong! Only time and empirical data will tell whether, or under what conditions, people will accept or reject such privacy threats as mandatory drug testing, workplace video monitoring, and e-commerce "leave behinds." To find out which way those cookies crumble, if indeed they will at all, we need a quantitative survey to assess our hunches, heuristics, and hypotheses about the supposed multiple manifestations of each value.

Steps 2 to 4

To fully understand the Environics socio-cultural system, one must spend some time learning how it is that we create operational measures of each value identified in the qualitative phase, and then how we analyze these together in multivariate (or multiple variable) space to create our maps. Again, we draw on both the work of other social scientists and our own empirical research to understand how best to assess each value and to explore the meaning of these values working in concert within each culture.

The first quantitative stage in the analysis is a familiar one in survey research: to develop and administer a high-quality survey to a representative sampling of the society's population so that valid inferences can be drawn, robust data patterns can be replicated, and confident generalizations can be made about various subgroups in the population. This requires steps 2 to 4 in our list above. The goal is to translate the subtle and not-so-subtle values and mental postures we sensed in the first step into a set of empirical measures that are valid and reliable, replicable and defensible. This is where science and art really begin to commingle in our work, and where, if we're any good at what we do, the solid scientific methodology underlying our values measurement system will be artfully conceived, crafted, and carried off.

Steps 5 to 7

Steps 5 to 7 represent the heart of the analysis. It's here that we both validate our hypothesized social values and discover new values that emerge from the data, using a multivariate statistical technique called principal components analysis (PCA) combined with Cronbach alpha reliability analysis. At the end of these steps we hope to have articulated a set of social values that adequately describes the culture under investigation and from which meaningful and interesting insights can be drawn. For the United States, we typically assess and track well over a hundred such values, from those with grand and enduring sociological stature, such as the *Need for Status Recognition, Obedience to Authority,* and *Sexism,* to those that describe the more subtle, immediate concerns of living, such as *Concern for Appearance, Meaningful Moments,* and *Discerning Hedonism.* Through such disparate content we are best able to capture people's mental, emotional, spiritual, and behavioural expectations and response tendencies, and thus to discern the phenomenology of their everyday lives.

Each value comprises the measurement and combination of several survey items in its construction. For example, *Global Consciousness* is defined as considering oneself a "citizen of the world" first and foremost over a "citizen of one's community and country," combined with a certain degree of non-ethnocentricity or feeling of affinity to peoples in all countries. This idea is measured by having respondents agree or disagree on a four-point scale with several items in the survey, such as "I feel that I am more a citizen of the world than a citizen of my country." The items are combined mathematically to create this value measure, scores are assigned to each respondent, and those respondents scoring highest (or sometimes lowest) on the value are classified as strong (or weak) in evidencing that tendency.

Steps 8 to 9

In steps 8 and 9, we again use principal components analysis (PCA), or sometimes factor analysis of correspondence (FAC), to explore the associations between individuals' standing on their many social values. From this analysis emerges a "map space solution," a set of axes or dimensions that more generally underlie, differentiate, and explain the collection of values we've assessed among our respondents. Many such solutions are possible and considered. The axes chosen should allow us to interpret the values together on one common map, to explore their positions relative to other values, and to track their movements through time in a compelling way. The axes are named to capture the main themes of the values and mental postures that define them. While there are usually three to seven axes that best describe the interrelations among the hundred-plus values we've assessed in our respondents, we typically depict the data in only the two most explanatory and interesting dimensions when explicating our findings.

It's important to remember that our map is about the *people* who are plotted there. Individuals are assigned a set of axis coordinates on the various dimensions, and we use these to plot either each individual, or the average positions of subgroups, or the entire population average of a culture, or of that culture at a specific point in time. The axes are chosen, in part, if the anchoring provided by plotting major demographic subgroups makes fundamental sense across the values space (for example, older age should be associated with greater conformity, and higher education with autonomy). But this isn't our sole criterion for selecting the axes.

Any type of group, demographic or not, can be defined and plotted on the map; as, for example,

- teenagers
- working women
- high-household-income earners
- Midwesterners
- generational cohorts, such as baby boomers
- supporters of a political party or position
- early adopters of a technology
- heavy Brand X users
- "somewhat dissatisfied" customers
- dog owners
- strong believers in the value *Ethical Consumerism*

The last example is of particular interest. In order to create the map that positions the hundred-plus social values, we place the name of each value we assess at the point on the map where its strongest proponents reside. We define "strongest proponents" as approximately the top fifth of people who report that they agree with the value (as assessed by all its items combined). In other words, the label "Ethical Consumerism" is positioned on the map by proxy, at the average axes position points of those 20 percent of individuals strongest in their orientation toward this value, which we arrive at by asking how much they monitor their consumption and buy from companies with good track records in environmental and employee practice.

Each of the groups listed above can also be profiled in terms of *all* their values to see what their particularly strong and weak value orientations are among the hundred-plus we assess. A complex array of value standings usually characterizes any one subgroup of interest—for example, the highly educated—but in total they must combine to give the group's average position on our two major values axes. In our proprietary work, we compute a set of scores for all hundred-plus values that indexes how much stronger or weaker a chosen group is on each of those values when compared with the national average (or any other comparison group of interest). The resulting gestalt of correlated value orientations for that group provides a rich portrait that can be used for understanding and communicating with them.

As explained in the body of this book, our analysis of America has revealed several major structural axes that can be used to describe the values of its citizens, of which the most important two are

- survival versus fulfillment
- authority versus individuality

These axes capture the organization of the values we assess when we consider them as a whole, and the resulting quadrants of this map provide a good description of the major *structure* of the values shared by a people. That notable movements have occurred in the past decade on each of these axes also makes them very useful in telling the *dynamic* story of social values evolution in America.

As we've seen in this book's central thesis, we can plot the evolutions and trajectories of the entire society and of subcultures through time on our map. The position points of such groups (certain voters, youth, the religious right, Hispanics) can be examined on the map as their values shift through time, and their group profiles can be studied over the years to describe the changes in their overall social values portraits.

The axes framework we've developed for the United States has been further enhanced by comparison of our work with ongoing qualitative and quantitative research studies conducted worldwide that probe the evolution of values and their meaning in many other cultures. We can describe not only the specific values that differentiate societies but also the commonalities that bind all peoples in the human experience. The axes of social change that emerge from our analysis of America are congruent with those that social scientists have discerned in studying cultures on other continents as well—an encouraging conceptual replication of our work that, despite local variations in history, politics, religion, and social forms, speaks to the universality of human values and to the common set of life challenges we face as members of our species.

Step 10

Once the primary map is set for a culture, our fun really begins. For it's in step 10 that we get to use our map for understanding people's values in much more depth, and for helping the people who pay the bills—our clients—do so. There are typically many surprises as we plumb the depths of people's world views and motivations, and much subtlety as well.

What do men and women have in common in social values, how are they different, and how are they changing? What are the values and world views associated with achieving a higher level of education? What are the in-depth values profiles of old people and young people, New Englanders and Texarkanians, professionals and unionists, Catholics and Protestants? What are the differences in mental postures of people who vote Democrat or Republican, jog versus bird-watch in their spare time, buy Toyotas versus Fords, drink Coke versus Pepsi, read *The New Yorker* versus *Maxim,* believe in angels or are atheists, run PCs versus Macs? What does the wider study of values tell us about the people in our society who are most accepting of violence, who are opting for voluntary simplicity in their lifestyles, or who are highly entrepreneurial?

Social values provide clues to each of these questions, and many, many more. Perhaps our system's greatest contribution comes from its ability to identify the basic mindsets that are emerging in our culture as well as globally. Are these the mindsets we should be teaching our children to prepare them for this new millennium? We think yes, but such a self-laudatory statement about "our contribution" is possible only if, like us, you judge *Adaptive Navigation* to be a desirable means of living and of charting the course to your goals in life.

Glossary of Values

ACCEPTANCE OF VIOLENCE   People highest on this trend believe that violence is an inevitable fact of life that must be accepted with a certain degree of indifference. Belief that violence can be both cathartic and persuasive.

ACKNOWLEDGMENT OF RACISM   Acknowledging that racism not only exists, but that Americans should make amends to African Americans and other minorities who have been discriminated against in the past. Belief that systemic racism has held African Americans back.

ACTIVE GOVERNMENT   Tendency to believe that government efficaciously performs socially beneficial functions. A desire for more government involvement in resolving social issues.

ADAPTABILITY TO COMPLEXITY   Tendency to adapt easily to the uncertainties of modern life and not feel threatened by the changes and complexities of society today. A desire to explore this complexity as a learning experience and a source of opportunity.

ADAPTIVE NAVIGATION   Having the flexibility to adapt to unforeseen events that interfere with the realization of one's goals. Being flexible in defining one's expectations and ways of meeting one's objectives.

ADVERTISING AS STIMULUS   Tendency to enjoy viewing advertising for its aesthetic properties; to enjoy advertising in a wide range of venues, from magazines to television to outdoor signs and billboards.

AMERICAN DREAM   The belief that the United States is the "land of opportunity" and that anyone can make it, and make it big, if they try hard enough. The belief that even in middle age one can start anew, launching new initiatives or changing one's way of life.

AMERICAN ENTITLEMENT A belief that all Americans deserve the ample material wealth they enjoy and shouldn't feel guilty about it. Believing that Americans shouldn't have to compromise their nation's interests or their standard of living for the benefit of others in the world.

ANOMIE AND AIMLESSNESS The feeling of having no goals in life. Experiencing a void of meaning with respect to life in general. A feeling of alienation from society, having the impression of being cut off from what's happening.

ATTRACTION TO CROWDS Enjoyment of being in large crowds as a means of de-individualization and connection-seeking.

AVERSION TO COMPLEXITY A desire to keep one's life simple and predictable. People strong on this trend are intimidated and threatened by the changes in society and the complexities of modern life. They seek stability and simplicity.

BRAND APATHY Placing little importance on the brand name of a product.

BUYING ON IMPULSE Tendency to purchase products on impulse, enticed by exciting advertising or packaging. Rarely seeking out information on products before buying.

CELEBRATING PASSAGES A need to perform certain rituals or small acts to demarcate the passing of various phases of one's life. A desire to celebrate traditional passages (e.g., birth, marriage, death) or invent new ones.

CIVIC APATHY Reflects a disinterest in the political process and participation in the democratic process. Recognition of the division of society between the "haves" and the "have nots," and a willingness to accept the inevitability of the status quo.

CIVIC ENGAGEMENT A belief that active involvement in the political process can make a difference in society. People strongest on this trend reject the notion that inequities in society are inevitable and should be expected.

COMMUNITY INVOLVEMENT Measure of the interest in what's happening in one's neighbourhood, city, town, or region. Reflected in activities ranging from reading the weekly community newspaper to socio-political involvement in community organizations.

CONCERN FOR APPEARANCE Placing a great deal of importance on appearing "attractive" and concerned about the image projected by one's appearance. People who are strong on this trend are image driven.

CONFIDENCE IN ADVERTISING   Tendency to trust and use advertising as a source of reliable information. Also, a tendency to identify with the fashions and the role models promoted by advertising and the consumer society.

CONFIDENCE IN BIG BUSINESS   The belief that big businesses strive to strike a fair balance between making a profit and working in the public's interest. Expressing a certain level of faith that what serves the interest of big business also serves the interest of society, and vice versa. Associating good quality and service with big companies and well-known products.

CONFIDENCE IN SMALL BUSINESS   Confidence in the commitment of small-business owners to the provision of quality goods and services. Belief that small-business owners aren't just profit driven.

CONFORMITY TO NORMS   A desire to conform to existing social norms. People strongest on this trend express concern about what others might think of them and make efforts to avoid standing out from others.

CONSISTENT SELF   Remaining true to one's own ideals and convictions, even in the face of social pressure. People who are strongest on this trend don't feel compelled to modify their beliefs, attitudes, or behaviour to conform to different social situations.

CRUDE MATERIALISM   Placing great importance on the accumulation of material possessions. Feeling a need to constantly buy new products and services.

CULTURAL ASSIMILATION   *E Pluribus Unum*. Belief that people should adopt a culture that is "American" first and foremost. Believing that in coming to America, immigrants should let go of their languages and customs and embrace the American way of life.

CULTURE SAMPLING   The belief that other cultures have a great deal to teach us, and the inclination to incorporate some of these cultural influences into one's own life.

DECONSUMPTION   The willingness to adopt a lifestyle in which consumption plays a less dominant role. This attitude is expressed in a desire to limit or reduce one's consumption of goods and to spend less than before.

DISCERNING HEDONISM   The capacity to savour pleasures; the appreciation of complex emotions and the ability to link enjoyment to other realms of experience in everyday life.

DISCOUNT CONSUMERISM   Preferring to buy discount or private-label brands, often from wholesalers, discount outlet stores, or the sale displays at national retailers.

DISCRIMINATING CONSUMERISM   Seeking objective, comparative product information and carefully evaluating one's needs before making purchases. Preference for practical and functional products that satisfy real needs.

DUTY   Belief that duties and obligations to others should be fulfilled before turning to one's personal pleasures and interests.

ECOLOGICAL CONCERN (REVERSE OF ECOLOGICAL FATALISM)   A tendency to believe that today's environmental problems are a result of industrial and personal disregard for the environment. These people feel that the trend toward environmental destruction is unacceptable and reject the notion that job protection or economic advancement should be allowed at the expense of environmental protection.

ECOLOGICAL FATALISM   People highest on this trend believe that some amount of pollution is unavoidable in industrial societies and accept it as a part of life. They feel there's little they can do to change this fact.

EFFORT TOWARD HEALTH   The commitment to focus on diet and exercise in order to feel better and have a healthy, wholesome lifestyle. A willingness to transform one's lifestyle through exercise and radical changes to diet.

EMOTIONAL CONTROL   A propensity to give priority to reason as the principal way of understanding life. A desire to keep one's emotional life on an even keel, to use logic and reason to control one's feelings and emotions and to base day-to-day decisions on reason and logic. A reluctance to experience or express emotions.

ENTHUSIASM FOR CONSUMPTION   Displaying an enthusiastic attitude toward consumption. Consumers strong on this trend intend to buy as much or more than they did before. They like to explore the marketplace and are always on the lookout for whatever is new on the market.

ENTHUSIASM FOR NEW TECHNOLOGY   Fascination with the possibilities offered by modern technology. Seeks information about the latest products and innovations. Excitement about the ways technology can better their lives.

ENTREPRENEURIALISM   Taking steps to fulfill the dream of becoming self-employed, rather than a nine-to-five employee. Feeling that the freedom and opportunity that come with owning one's own business is more rewarding than working for someone else.

EQUAL RELATIONSHIP WITH YOUTH   Breaking down traditional hierarchical and patriarchal relationships by giving youth freedoms equal to those of adults. Discipline as issued by adults over young people is therefore replaced by freedom and increased individualism.

ETHICAL CONSUMERISM   A focus on the perceived ethical and social-responsibility policies and practices of the companies from which one buys. Consideration of labour policies, mistreatment of animals, etc. Desire to see companies be good corporate citizens in terms of these social concerns.

EVERYDAY ETHICS   A measure of how individuals respond in situations that put their ethical beliefs to the test. When they see a way of turning a situation to their advantage at the expense of another person, institution, or company, how does they respond? Will they report mistakes made in their favour by a waiter, a bank, or the government?

EVERYDAY RAGE   A willingness to express anger and dissatisfaction toward others. This ranges from a refusal to accept bad service to arguing with others in public or even engaging in road rage. Implicit in this is a feeling that people can no longer expect fair treatment by being polite or quiet.

FAITH IN SCIENCE   The belief that science and technology can work in a positive way by expanding natural resources to meet future demand, and that new technologies can repair past damage to the natural world. Excitement about the possibilities offered by new technologies and modern medicine.

FATALISM   The tendency to believe that one's life is shaped by forces beyond one's control. Feeling unconcerned about trying to change the inevitable direction of one's life.

FEAR OF VIOLENCE   Fear of violence occurring in today's society. Feeling insecure about personal safety, feeling vulnerable to attack in the city or in one's neighbourhood, especially at night. Tendency to believe that one must be on constant alert against gratuitous violence.

FINANCIAL SECURITY   A feeling of security and optimism about one's financial future. A sense of being personally responsible for and in control of one's financial situation.

FLEXIBLE FAMILIES   Willingness to accept non-traditional definitions of family, such as common-law and same-sex marriages. The belief that family should be defined by emotional links rather than by legal formalities or institutions. The belief that society should be open to new definitions of what constitutes a family.

FLEXIBLE GENDER IDENTITY (REVERSE OF TRADITIONAL GENDER IDENTITY)   The feeling that one has both a feminine and masculine side to one's personality. The desire to actively explore and express these different facets of one's personality. Having a feeling of being more masculine at times and more feminine at others.

GENDER PARITY   Seeking fairness and equal treatment for men and women in work roles. A desire to transcend sexual stereotypes and to see an end to discrimination, tempered by a belief that a job should go to the best candidate, man or woman, rather than employing reverse discrimination to achieve equal representation of men and women in all professions.

GLOBAL CONSCIOUSNESS   Considering oneself a "citizen of the world" first and foremost over a "citizen of one's community and country." Non-ethnocentricity; feeling affinity to peoples in all countries.

HETERARCHY   Tendency to think that leadership in organizations should be flexible and fluid, that a single leader shouldn't take control of everything, and that initiatives and leadership should emerge from different individuals as a function of their strengths. A belief that teamwork is more effective than autocracy.

HOLISTIC HEALTH   Taking a holistic approach to health and well-being. Individuals who are high on this trend are sensitive to the linkage between their mental, spiritual, and physical well-being. They feel they can exert control over their health, and that the choices they make today will pay off in later years.

IMPORTANCE OF AESTHETICS   Tendency to base purchase decisions on aesthetic rather than utilitarian considerations. Measures the attention given to the beauty of objects and products purchased. People strong on this trend often buy products purely for their appearance.

IMPORTANCE OF BRAND   Giving great weight to the brand name of a product or service; a tendency to have favourite brands.

IMPORTANCE OF SPONTANEITY   Tendency to enthusiastically embrace the unexpected and spontaneous events that temporarily interrupt daily routines.

INTEREST IN THE UNEXPLAINED   Tendency to reject the assumption that all valid knowledge must be logical, rational, or scientific in favour of an acceptance of beliefs or phenomena that remain mysterious or unexplained by modern science.

INTROSPECTION AND EMPATHY   Tendency to analyze and examine one's actions and those of others, rather than being judgmental about variances from the norm or from one's own way of doing things. An interest in understanding life rather than taking sides.

INTUITION AND IMPULSE   A way of understanding and engaging with the world that largely leaves aside controlled and critical rational thought. A tendency to be guided less by reason and ideology than by one's own emotions and feelings. Impulsive and spontaneous; able to change one's opinions easily.

JOY OF CONSUMPTION   Intense gratification through the purchase of consumer goods (rather than basic necessities). Enjoying consumption for the pleasure of consumption. People who are strong on this trend are often more excited by the act of buying than by the use of the products they buy.

JUST DESERTS   Confidence that, in the end, people get what they deserve as a result of the decisions they make, both positively and negatively.

LARGESSE OBLIGE   Social conscience of the economic variety. The "haves" have a moral duty to help or share with the "have nots."

LIVING VIRTUALLY   People strong on this trend are spending an increasing amount of time watching TV, using computers, or at the movies. Reflects a more virtual than real connection to the world.

LOOK GOOD FEEL GOOD   A belief that, by taking care to look one's best, one will feel and project confidence, thereby helping to achieve one's goals in life.

MALLEABLE SELF   Social chameleonism; feeling the need to adapt to different social settings by modifying one's beliefs, attitudes, and behaviours. Having few strongly held convictions that are maintained in the face of social pressure.

MEANINGFUL MOMENTS   Cherishing the ordinary moments in everyday life over once-in-a-lifetime, grand-scale events. Taking time to indulge in individual pleasures. The sense of impermanence that accompanies momentary connections with others doesn't diminish the value of the moment.

MODERN RACISM   A modern definition of racism based on the belief that racism is largely a thing of the past and that African Americans in particular have gained more than they deserve.

MORE POWER FOR BUSINESS   Belief that business institutions (e.g., banks, foreign companies) should have a greater influence in society.

MORE POWER FOR MEDIA   Belief that celebrities and those in the media should have a greater influence in society.

MORE POWER FOR POLITICS   Belief that government institutions and political parties should have a greater influence in society.

MULTICULTURALISM   Openness toward the diverse cultures, ethnic communities, and immigrants that make up America. A belief that ethnic groups should be encouraged to preserve their cultural identities, and that others should seek to learn about them.

MYSTERIOUS FORCES   The impression that forces greater than ourselves control our destiny and that mysterious forces that we cannot understand affect our lives.

NATIONAL PRIDE   Defining one's identity through national pride and believing that America should hold a strong position in the world.

NEED FOR STATUS RECOGNITION   Desire to be held in esteem and respect by others, and to express one's social standing or aspired status through a display of fine manners, good taste, "class," or "chic."

NEED FOR UNIQUENESS   A desire to be individualistic and stand out in the crowd. People strongest on this trend don't worry about what others might think of them but tailor their appearance, behaviour, and activities to be different.

NETWORKING   The desire to assemble a diverse network of friends and associations based on one's own personal interests. Often these friends and associations will have little in common apart from the fact that they're all connected to one's own interests.

OBEDIENCE TO AUTHORITY   A belief in playing by the rules. The belief that persons or organizations in positions of authority should be deferred to at all times. There are rules in society and everyone should follow them. Feeling that young people in particular should be taught to obey authority rather than question it.

OSTENTATIOUS CONSUMPTION   Desire to impress others and express one's social standing through the display of objects that symbolize affluence.

PAROCHIALISM   Feeling of connectedness to one's town, city, region, or country. A disregard for what's happening in other countries, and a preference for seeing symbols of home, such as a McDonald's restaurant, when travelling abroad.

PATRIARCHY   Belief that "the father of the family must be the master in his own home."

PENCHANT FOR RISK   Desire to take risks in order to get what one wants out of life. Also, indulging in dangerous and forbidden activities for their associated emotional high.

PERSONAL CHALLENGE   Setting difficult goals, even if just to prove to themselves that they can do it. People strong on this trend finish what they start, persevering until their self-assigned task is completed to their satisfaction. Rejecting personal failure.

PERSONAL CONTROL   Striving to organize and control the direction of one's future, even when it feels that there are forces beyond one's immediate control.

PERSONAL CREATIVITY   Desire to use one's imagination and creative talents in daily life, both at work and at play.

PERSONAL ESCAPE   Interest in mystery, romanticism, and adventure as a means of distracting oneself from everyday challenges and burdens. People strongest on this trend feel that their dreams and imagination are important driving forces in their daily lives; they long for that which is beyond the practical and desire to experience beauty and pleasure in surprise and astonishment.

PERSONAL EXPRESSION   The desire to develop and express one's personality, combined with a desire to communicate in an authentic and sincere manner with others.

PRIMACY OF THE FAMILY   Centrality of family; making personal sacrifices and providing for one's children over all else.

PROPRIETY   The importance of dressing so as not to give offence but rather to elicit and communicate respect in more formal relationships, in public, and at work. Behaving in a way that respects oneself and others. A preference for the formal over the casual.

PROTECTION OF PRIVACY   Great concern about the fact that in databases, among other ways, government and business are amassing increasingly large banks of information about people's private lives.

PURSUIT OF INTENSITY   Desire to live intensely. Also, a tendency to be guided less by reason and ideology than by one's own emotions, feelings, and intuition. A need to constantly experience new sensations.

RACIAL FUSION   People who are strongest on this trend are accepting of ethnic diversity within families, such as interracial marriage, believing that it enriches people's lives.

REJECTION OF AUTHORITY   Desire to transcend the rigid framework of traditional authority. Possessing a questioning orientation, critical of and willing to look beyond the status quo.

REJECTION OF ORDER   Living with a certain amount of disorder as an expression of oneself. Also, a desire to distance oneself from society's traditional moral code governing good manners and the golden rule in favour of a more informal and relaxed approach to life.

RELIGION À LA CARTE   A selective, personal, adaptive, and eclectic approach to the adoption of religious beliefs. Spiritually questing, seeking personal fulfillment through learning about other faiths.

RELIGIOSITY   Placing great importance on religion as a construct that guides one's life. Also, placing great significance on having an affiliation with an organized religious faith. Tendency to consider religion as representing the essential values and education that should be transmitted to the next generation.

REVERSE SEXISM   Belief that women, not men, are the superior gender. Feeling that women are more adaptable and intelligent than men, better equipped to function in the modern world.

SAVING ON PRINCIPLE   The tendency to save and accumulate money, motivated by a moral impulse for future security. A preference for frugality and denial to self of "luxuries." Displaying tendencies toward inhibition.

SEARCH FOR ROOTS   Desire to preserve and maintain one's cultural and ethnic roots and to live in accordance with one's own traditions and customs. Also, a yearning to return to one's cultural roots in order to rediscover, and participate in, the fundamental values that give meaning to one's life.

SELECTIVE USE OF PERSONAL SERVICES   Deferring to experts for advice when needed, but maintaining contact with them. Those highest on this trend seek opportunities to learn from them or even to play an active role in the decision-making process.

SENSUALISM   Tendency to give priority to the sensory perceptions aroused by the non-visual senses. A more sensual, intuitive, and affective approach to life.

SEXISM   Belief that "the father of the family must be the master in his own home." Believing in traditional, male-dominated views on the division of gender roles—that men are naturally superior to women. These views carry into economic issues, such as the belief that when both partners are working the husband should be the main breadwinner.

SEXUAL PERMISSIVENESS   A tendency to be sexually permissive regarding oneself and others. Fidelity within marriage or between partners and the prohibition of premarital sex are of little importance.

SKEPTICISM OF ADVERTISING   Distrust that advertising messages are truthful or even helpful for making purchasing decisions.

SOCIAL INTIMACY   A desire to be around and connect with smaller, closely knit groups of people. Feeling that smaller organizations are better than larger ones.

SOCIAL MOBILITY   Feeling that social advancement is both desirable and available to those with the skills and/or connections to make it happen. Reliance on such "hard skills" as education and training, as well as such "soft skills" as using personal relations to advance.

SOCIAL RESPONSIBILITY   A belief that society and the individual have a responsibility to help those less fortunate. Tendency to believe that quality of life can improve when people work together.

SPIRITUAL QUEST   A desire for an intense spiritual life, contemplating questions of existence and meaning.

STATUS VIA HOME   Feeling a strong sense that one's home represents an extension of one's image. People strongest on this trend make great efforts to decorate and equip their homes in a manner that will impress others, and pay particular attention to the way they entertain in the home.

STRATEGIC CONSUMPTION   An attitude adopted by consumers to get the best price for whatever they buy. The methods vary and can include, for example, making a better assessment of their needs in order to be more selective in their purchases, hunting for special promotions, discounts, bargains or other forms of price reduction, switching to cheaper brands, and postponing purchases.

TECHNOLOGY ANXIETY   People strong on this trend are intimidated and threatened by technological changes and express high concern about the ethical and moral dimensions toward which science is advancing.

TIME STRESS   Feeling overwhelmed by the demands on one's time. A desire to obtain better control of one's life stress, particularly as it applies to better time management.

TRADITIONAL FAMILY   Defining family in traditional terms as a man and a woman, married with children. Unwilling to expand the traditional concept of family beyond the legal formality of a marriage licence to include same-sex or unmarried couples.

TRADITIONAL GENDER IDENTITY   The belief that normal gender behaviour is clearly delineated—men are masculine and women are feminine—and that particular characteristics are inherent in gender. The rejection of the notion that masculine and feminine behaviour and roles can, or should, cross the traditional gender line.

UPSCALE CONSUMERISM   Preferring to buy mostly exclusive or prestigious brands that are more expensive and often available only from higher-end stores and boutiques.

VITALITY   The sense that one has a great deal of energy and is in contact with this energy. Measures an energetic, lively approach to life; a feeling that one has more vigour and initiative than most other people.

VOLUNTARY SIMPLICITY   Balancing quality versus quantity in life. The desire to achieve a sense of quality of life combined with the willingness to scale back one's material expectations or concentrate on those things that are truly important in life.

WORK ETHIC   Following the golden rule and guiding one's life according to the principle of deferring pleasure in order to realize greater gains in the future. Individuals who score high on this trend believe that children should be taught to work hard in order to get ahead.

XENOPHOBIA   The sense that too much immigration threatens the purity of the country. The belief that immigrants who've made their new home in the United States should set aside their cultural backgrounds and blend into the American melting pot.

Complete Display of Values by Quadrant

THE STATUS AND SECURITY QUADRANT

AUTHORITY

Religiosity

Everyday Ethics

Duty

Meaningful Moments

American Dream

Effort Toward Health
Social Responsability
Emotional Control
Social Intimacy

Cultural Assimilation

Holistic Health
Consistent Self
Discriminating Consumption
Civic Engagement

Discount Consumerism

Mysterious Forces
Deconsumption
Strategic Consumption
Introspection & Empathy

FULFILLMENT

THE IDEALISM AND AUTONOMY QUADRANT

FULFILLMENT

Brand Apathy

Need for Uniqueness

Importance of Spontaneity

Interest in the Unexplained

Skepticism Toward Advertising

Flexible Gender Identity

Rejection of Authority

Flexible Families

INDIVIDUALITY

THE EXCLUSION AND INTENSITY QUADRANT

SURVIVAL

Fatalism   Joy of Consumption

Attraction for Crowds

Financial Security

Just Deserts   Enthusiasm for New Technology Personal Escape

Crude Materialism   Adaptability to Complexity

Interest in the Unexplained

Ostentatious Consumption

Enthusiasm for Consumption

Malleable Self

Pursuit of Intensity

Upscale Consumerism   Buying on Impulse

Anomie-Aimlessness   Racial Fusion

Acceptance of Violence   Penchant for Risk

Sexual Permissiveness

Equal Relationship with Youth

INDIVIDUALITY

THE STATUS AND SECURITY QUADRANT

AUTHORITY

Traditional Family

Obedience to Authority

Work Ethic
Traditional Gender Identity

Selective Use of Professional Services

Patriarchy   Discerning Hedonism

Fear of Violence

American Entitlement

Protection of Privacy

Technology Anxiety   Look Good, Feel Good

Celebrating Passages

Confidence in Small Business

Xenophobia   Confidence in Advertising   Aversion to Complexity

SURVIVAL

Advertising as Stimulus   Social Mobility   Vitality

Saving on Principle   Adaptive Navigation

Notes

INTRODUCTION

1. Sociologist Alan Wolfe sensed that polling wasn't enough. So in *One Nation, After All*, he conducted prolonged interviews with a cross-section of 200 middle-class Americans of different races, regions, and religions, and concluded that at bottom, Americans basically agree on many supposedly divisive issues (gay rights was the one marked exception). I believe Wolfe had the right idea; his sampling was thoughtful and his book is fascinating. But however carefully conducted, a one-time survey of such a small number has obvious limitations, as Wolfe acknowledges.

2. One important exception to this patter is the World Values Survey (WVS), directed by Ron Inglehart of the University of Michigan's political science department. Since 1981, the WVS has amassed thousands of surveys of eighty societies from around the world; one of these societies is the United States. While the WVS tends to focus on cross-cultural comparison, 2005 will see the release of *America's Crisis of Values*, a book by sociologist Wayne Baker based on WVS data.

3. Our methodology is discussed in greater detail at the end of the Introduction, and is laid barer still in Appendix A.

4. Laura Miller, "Self-help Nation," *Salon*, 23 August 2005.

5. Although we construct most of our own questions, some items in our battery are drawn from published scales in sociology, psychology, and political science. This is not an academic work, and it does not describe all academic influences on our apparatus, but those desiring further information about our battery and/or methodology are invited to contact Environics' Advanced Analytics department.

6. More information on the construction of the social values map is available in Appendix A.

ONE: RETRENCHMENT AND RENEWAL

1. Divorce: The Census Bureau has state-level divorce rates for forty-six states in 2001. If these states are ranked from the highest to the lowest divorce rates,

the top half includes just three blue states and twenty red states. Crime: If we similarly rank the states according to crime rates (2003 FBI data), there are just four blue states in the top half (twenty-five) of the property crime rankings, compared with sixteen in the bottom half. On violent crime we find eight blue states in the top half, compared with twelve blue states in the bottom half. Unmarried Birth Rates: A similar ranking of the states on unmarried births (National Vital Statistics Reports, 2002 data) finds seven blue states in the top half and thirteen in the bottom half. Of the ten states with the highest unmarried birth rates, only one (Delaware) is blue.

2. Certainly, some particularly frothy Republican pundits may disingenuously overstate the extent to which they actually attribute America's (or the world's) ills to Democrats, but I'm speaking here of politicians and ordinary Americans who see themselves as earnestly engaged in a culture war.

3. Our values map contains a trend labelled *Introspection and Empathy*, which falls very near the right extreme of the map.

4. The reasons for this decline, underway since the 1970s, confuse criminologists, who cannot link it consistently to incarceration rates, economic cycles, policing practices, or any other explanation. One highly controversial theory, offered by economist Steven Levitt in his book *Freakonomics* (co-authored by Stephen Dubner), attributes diminished crime in recent decades to increased abortion rates in the foregoing decades. Because abortions became more readily available, the argument goes, those who would probably have been responsible for the bulk of crimes a couple of decades after they were born never *were* born—and thus their statistically probable crimes never took place.

5. Associated Press, "Lakewood Church Opens at New Home in Grand Fashion," 16 July 2005.

6. *Just Deserts* was measured only in 2000 and 2004.

7. Index scores are explained in the Introduction. Change scores work the same way, but instead of comparing the values of a group within society, such as Americans under age twenty, with the average of the whole society, they compare a society with itself at another time—in this case America in 2004 with America in 2000, and America in 2004 with America in 1992.

TWO: THE REAL CULTURE WAR: EITHER VERSUS NEITHER

1. Any numbers I offer on voter turnout refer to eligible voters (distinct from registered voters) and are provided by the Committee for the Study of the American Electorate at George Washington University. Our own question on voting intention, which I use in this chapter to divide Americans into groups according to political engagement, reads as follows: "What would you say are the chances that you will vote in the November 2004 election

for president? Are you almost certain to vote, will you probably vote, are the chances 50/50 or do you think that you will not vote?" The written survey then offers five boxes labelled "almost certain to vote," "probably will vote," "50/50 chance you will vote," "will not vote," and "ineligible to vote."

2. Throughout this section, references to Democrats and Republicans denote those who identify as Democrat or Republican *and* reported that they were certain to vote in the next election.

3. Bill Bishop, "Political Parties Now Rooted in Two Different Americas," *Austin American-Statesman,* 18 September 2004.

4. In these descriptions of the major demographic groups that skew Republican and Democratic, we use a combined data set from all four waves of our U.S. surveys: 1992, 1996, 2000, and 2004.

5. *The London Review,* 2 December 2004, p. 8.

6. Our formulation of this "progressive" group is explained in detail in the final chapter.

THREE: GENDER AND RACE

1. Press release from University of Michigan News Service, "U.S. Husbands Are Doing More Housework While Wives Are Doing Less," 12 March 2002.

2. The U.S. Census Bureau categorizes race and Hispanic origin separately, with Hispanic being defined by the Office of Management and Budget as "a person of Cuban, Mexican, Puerto Rican, South or Central American, or other Spanish culture or origin regardless of race." Thus, Hispanic is primarily a cultural category, not a racial one (one can be black and Hispanic, white and Hispanic, and so on). Whether the definition of the group is racial, cultural, or linguistic, it seems to me to make intuitive sense to discuss Hispanics as a group alongside blacks and whites, if only because convention treats them as such: politicians, marketers, and others speak about and to "Hispanics."

FOUR: REGION

1. The regional profiles in this chapter are based on all four waves of our surveys: '92, '96, '00, and '04. Of course this approach obscures change over time, but it offers the advantage of larger sample sizes and therefore more robust conclusions.

2. Montana, Idaho, Wyoming, Colorado, Utah, Nevada, New Mexico, Arizona.

3. New York, New Jersey, Pennsylvania, West Virginia.

4. Tennessee, Alabama, Mississippi.

5. Ohio, Kentucky, Michigan, Indiana, Wisconsin, Illinois.

6. Maine, Massachusetts, Vermont, New Hampshire, Connecticut, Rhode Island.

7. Washington, Oregon, California.

8. Minnesota, North Dakota, South Dakota, Iowa, Nebraska, Missouri, Kansas.

9. Delaware, DC, Maryland, Virginia, North Carolina, South Carolina, Florida, Georgia.

10. Texas, Oklahoma, Arkansas, Louisiana.

FIVE: THE GREAT BACKLASH

1. Valerie Bauerlein, "Jones Sails a Contrarian Course," *News and Observer*, 15 May 2005.

2. As John Micklethwaite and Adrian Wooldridge observe in their excellent book *The Right Nation: Conservative Power in America* (New York: Penguin, 2004), "The American Conservative Union tracks voting records of the members of the House of Representatives on the basis of loyalty to the conservative cause. In 1972, the average score for House Republicans was 63 percent; by 2002 it was 91 percent."

3. Rick Perlstein, *Before the Storm: Barry Goldwater and the Unmaking of the American Consensus* (New York: Hill and Wang, 2001), 13.

4. Micklethwaite and Wooldridge, *The Right Nation*.

5. David Frum, *The 70s* (Toronto: Random House Canada, 2000), 278.

6. Seymour Martin Lipset, *American Exceptionalism* (New York: W.W. Norton, 1996), 121.

7. History of the FHA, www.hud.gov/offices/hsg/fhahistory.cfm, accessed 24 January 2005.

8. Andres Duany, Elizabeth Plater-Zyberk, and Jeff Speck, *Suburban Nation: The Rise of Sprawl and the Decline of the American Dream* (New York: North Point Press, 2000).

9. David Brooks, *On Paradise Drive* (New York: Simon & Schuster, 2004).

10. M. Jeffrey Hardwick, *Mall Maker: Victor Gruen, Architect of an American Dream* (Philadelphia: University of Pennsylvania Press, 2004).

11. Tania Branigan, Luke Harding, and Owen Gibson, "Bush Says: I Put US Interests First," *The Guardian,* 4 July 2005.

12. Donald Rumsfeld, remarks on *Face the Nation*, CBS, 23 September 2001. Quoted in Jennifer Welsh, *At Home in the World* (Toronto: HarperCollins, 2004).

SIX: REACHING BEYOND THE CHOIR

1. Klein, Naomi. Interview. *Start Making Sense: Turning the Lessons of Election 2004 into Winning Progressive Politics.* Eds. Lakshmi Chaudry and Don Hazen. Vermont: Chelsea Green, 2005.

2. Morrison, Toni. "Clinton as the First Black President." *The New Yorker.* 12 October 1998.

3. These profiles should not be confused with the portraits offered in Chapter 2. Chapter 2 described the values of demographic groups tending to skew Democrat or Republican without regard to those people's actual reported political affiliations.

4. Of course, this indifference is self-reported. Status-seeking is arguably a universal human trait (at least in modern capitalist societies). So while progressives might claim not to be interested in impressing friends with their possessions, they may not be taking into account the baubles David Brooks so wonderfully describes in *Bobos in Paradise:* that slate shower stall *might* have been a spiritual acquisition, but friends know that it cost $20,000. Nevertheless, the fact that core progressives claim to reject consumption and status-seeking is significant, even if the rejection is only aspirational.

Bibliography

Albom, Mitch. "Homophobia Curtails Some Harmless Fun." *Detroit Free Press* 21 Nov. 2004.

American Beauty. Dir. Sam Mendes. Screenplay: Alan Ball. Dreamworks, 1999.

Annie Hall. Dir. Woody Allen. MGM, 1977.

Associated Press. "Lakewood Church Opens at New Home in Grand Fashion." 16 July 2005.

Baker, Wayne. *America's Crisis of Values: Reality and Perception.* Princeton: Princeton UP, 2005.

Bauerlein, Valerie. "Jones Sails a Contrarian Course." *News and Observer.* 15 May 2005.

Bishop, Bill. "Political Parties Now Rooted in Two Different Americas." *Austin American-Statesma*n 18 Sept. 2004.

Boswell, James. *Life of Johnson.* 1791. Toronto: Oxford UP, 1998.

Branigan, Tania, Luke Harding, and Owen Gibson. "Bush Says: I Put US Interests First." *The Guardian.* 4 July 2005.

Brooks, David. *On Paradise Drive.* New York: Simon and Schuster, 2004.

Buckley, Jr., William F. "Publisher's Statement." *National Review.* 19 Nov. 1955.

Cooper, Richard T. "General Casts War in Religious Terms." *Los Angeles Times.* 16 Oct. 2003.

Crossfire. CNN. 15 Oct. 2004.

de Vulpian, Alain. *À l'écoute des gens ordinaires : Comment ils transforment le monde.* Paris: Dunod, 2003.

"Dean Defendes View of GOP as 'Christian Party.'" *Associated Press.* 8 June 2005.

Du Bois, W.E.B. *The Souls of Black Folk.* 1903. New York: Penguin, 1996.

Duany, Andres, Elizabeth Plater-Zyberk, and Jeff Speck. *Suburban Nation: The Rise of Sprawl and the Decline of the American Dream.* NewYork: North Point Press, 2000.

"Due to 'Cross-Dressing' Fear, Students to Wear Camouflage." *Associated Press* 17 Nov. 2004.

Fight Club. Dir. David Fincher. Writing credits: Chuck Palahniuk (novel); Jim Uhls (screenplay). Fox, 1999.

Franti, Michael and Spearhead. "Stay Human." *Stay Human.* Boo Boo Wax and Six Degrees, 2001.

Freeman, Alan. "Nevada Voters Come Out for Bush and Brothels." *Globe and Mail.* 9 Nov. 2004.

Frum, David. *The 70s.* Toronto: Random House Canada, 2000.

Gladwell, Malcolm. *Blink: The Power of Thinking without Thinking.* New York: Little, Brown, 2005.

Goldberg, Jonah. "Rage against the Vote Rockers." *National Review Online.* 10 Mar. 2004.

Hardwick, M. Jeffrey. *Mall Maker: Victor Gruen, Architect of an American Dream.* Philadelphia: University of Pennsylvania Press, 2004.

Hertzberg, Hendrik. "In Moderation." *New Yorker.* 13 Sept. 2004.

Hunter, James Davison. *Culture Wars: The Struggle to Define America.* New York: Basic Books, 1991.

Huntington, Samuel P. *Who Are We? The Challenges to America's National Identity.* New York: Simon & Schuster, 2004.

Kaplan, Robert D. "Looking the World in the Eye." *Atlantic Monthly.* December, 2001.

Kirn, Walter. "What Color Is Montana?" *New York Times Magazine.* 2 Jan. 2005.

Klein, Naomi. Interview. *Start Making Sense: Turning the Lessons of Election 2004 into Winning Progressive Politics.* Eds. Lakshmi Chaudry and Don Hazen. Vermont: Chelsea Green, 2005.

Levitt, Steven D., and Stephen J. Dubner. *Freakonomics.* New York: HarperCollins, 2005.

Lieven, Anatol. "Taking Back America." *The London Review of Books.* 2 Dec. 2004.

Lipset, Seymour Martin. *American Exceptionalism.* New York: W.W. Norton, 1996.

Mahler, Jonathan. "The Soul of the New Exurb." *New York Times Magazine.* 27 Mar. 2005.

Maslow, A.H. *Toward a Psychology of Being.* Englewood Cliffs, NJ: Van Nostrand, 1962.

Micklethwait, John, and Adrian Wooldridge. *The Right Nation: Conservative Power in America.* New York: Penguin, 2004.

Miller, Laura. "Self-Help Nation." *Salon.* 23 Aug. 2005.

Morrison, Toni. "Clinton as the First Black President." *New Yorker.* 12 Oct. 1998.

NBC *News's Meet the Press*. NBC. 7 Nov. 2004.

O'Connor, Flannery. *Collected Stories*. New York: Farrar, Strauss, Giroux, 1996.

Perlstein, Rick. *Before the Storm: Barry Goldwater and the Unmaking of the American Consensus*. New York: Hill and Wang, 2001.

Putnam, Robert D. *Bowling Alone: The Collapse and Revival of American Community*. New York: Touchstone, 2000.

Rich, Frank. "How Dirty Harry Turned Commie." *New York Times* 13 Feb. 2005.

Rifkin, Jeremy. *The European Dream*. New York: Penguin, 2004.

———. "On 'Moral Values,' It's Blue in a Landslide." *New York Times* 14 Nov. 2004.

Rokeach, M. *Beliefs, Attitudes and Values*. San Francisco: Jossey-Bass, 1968.

———. *The Nature of Human Values*. New York: Free Press, 1973.

Rumsfeld, Donald. remarks on *Face the Nation*. CBS. 23 Sept. 2001. Quoted in Jennifer Welsh. *At Home in the World*. Toronto: HarperCollins, 2004.

Smiley, Shannon. "Sea of Youth Embraces New Pope." *Washington Post*. 22 Aug. 2005.

Tocqueville, Alexis de. *Democracy in America*. Chicago: University of Chicago Press, 2000.

Veblen, Thorstein. *Theory of the Leisure Class*. Toronto: Viking Penguin, 1994.

Wolfe, Alan. *One Nation, After All*. Toronto: Penguin, 1998.

Acknowledgments

THIS ACT OF HUBRIS would not have been possible without the collaboration of my two associates Amy Langstaff and David Jamieson.

My brilliant colleague Amy Langstaff was indispensable in this book's analysis and in its crafting. She is responsible for more than her fair share of the metaphors, similes, and cultural references that we hope bring life to this narrative and flow to its story. Dr. David Jamieson performed the statistical work creating the patterns that cried out for this book-length interpretation.

The three of us are also grateful to our colleagues at Environics: Barry Watson, David MacDonald, Kevin Shanahan, Susan Seto, and Phil Straforelli, who work in our social values consultancy, as well as our new colleagues in Oakland, California, Ted Nordhaus and Michael Shellenberger at American Environics, whose analysis of bridge values and constituencies of opportunity has greatly informed our work. A special thanks to our colleague Dan Lund, who from his office in Mexico City pored over this bold book about his native land and offered a plethora of useful comments and insights.

In turn, we all are grateful to our intellectual forebears, among whom are two remarkable Frenchmen. The first, Alexis de Tocqueville, author of the seminal *Democracy in America,* sits on the shoulders of anyone who is ever so hubristic as to attempt a portrait of the first new nation. The second, Alain de Vulpian, is the founding father of our research tradition. I would be remiss if I did not also acknowledge the great American political sociologist Seymour Martin Lipset, whose prodigious academic contributions have inspired me since I was assigned to read *Agrarian*

Socialism, The First New Nation, and *Political Man* as an undergraduate in the mid 1960s. Finally, my thanks to the two other founding fathers of our initial 1992 U.S. research, Larry Kaagan of New York and Alain Giguère of Montreal.

All of us of course are grateful to that intrepid interviewer who in 1992 conducted the first of the nearly 9,000 interviews that constitute the basic empirical facts of this research—and to her first respondent. That soul, perhaps living somewhere in Kansas, took the time to answer all our crazy questions while surely wondering what anyone might possibly learn from his responses.

Once again, I am thankful to have as my agent the formidable Bruce Westwood and as my publisher and editor respectively David Davidar and Diane Turbide of Penguin Group (Canada). Encouragement and wise counsel from each of these three made the heavy lifting a little lighter. Copy editor Karen Alliston also went a long way to making all this data readable.

To each of these folks and a myriad more, Amy, Dave, and I owe our deepest thanks.

Index

Page numbers in italics indicate illustrative text. Some text in italics refers to values and trends (eg. Acceptance of Violence; Acknowledgment of Racism; Ostentatious Consumption). References to notes are followed by n.